P9-AOD-086

Basic Concepts in Christian Pedagogy

BASIC CONCEPTS IN CHRISTIAN PEDAGOGY

Jan Waterink

Professor of Education and Psychology
Free University of Amsterdam

THE CALVIN FOUNDATION LECTURES
FOR 1954

WM. B. EERDMANS PUBLISHING COMPANY

Grand Rapids 1954 Michigan

Set up and printed, June, 1954

PRINTED IN THE UNITED STATES OF AMERICA

Contents

Basic Concepts in Christian Pedagogy

1

Foundations of Christian Pedagogics

PERHAPS it will seem unusual to speak of the foundations of Christian pedagogics. For one might ask: Is it not true that every school of pedagogics is founded on the same principles? Indeed, pedagogics is the theory of education and one may freely concede that a Christian education is different from a humanistic one. But does it follow that the foundations of a science change as the views according to which this science is put into practice are modified?

Furthermore, it is open to question whether pedagogics is generally regarded as a science. In writing about the "International Congress for Teaching Educational Sciences in Universities" at Ghent, in the Scottish *Educational Journal* of October 23, 1953, Norman T. Walker makes the following observations:

> Professor Campbell Stewart, in opening the discussion on British practice, remarked that the expression, education sciences, is not much used in this country. Nor can it be said that there emerged any clearly formulated concept of a "science" of education from the contributions of the various speakers. While there are naturally wide differences between countries, the general trend of development is that of education as a subject of University study emerging slowly from its subordination within the department of Philosophy (as a sort of *philosophia minor*) and asserting its claims to independence of other disciplines.

This observation defines the existing situation rather well, though somewhat optimistically, for pedagogy frequently presents itself as if it were merely applied psychology.

Accordingly, we are immediately confronted with the question as to whether pedagogy is a science. And if so, how is it related to practical education on the one hand; and on the other, to what extent do the principles, upon which the practice of education is based, affect the science of education?

At the outset, therefore, we must consider the following questions: (1) May the theory of education properly be regarded as a science? (2) In what way are the theory and practice of education influenced by principles? And finally, if there is such an influence, (3) What are the basic principles of Christian padagogics?

Undoubtedly the questions as to whether there is such a thing as a science of education and whether pedagogy truly is a science cannot be separated from the question as to what is our concept of education. At this very point already we are concerned with principles. Therefore, we should start by regarding the question as to whether pedagogy is a science in the light of the principles upon which our position is based. It is one thing to believe that education merely consists in the removal of obstacles so that the child will be able to follow his natural tendencies, thereby giving free scope for the realization of inherited traits in society. Needless to say, it is quite another thing to regard education as the guiding of human beings in such a manner that they with their talents will be able rightly to serve God, their creator, in the society in which they have been placed.

This suggests at once the question whether or not the concept of education implies the concept of a "norm." Is the purpose of education merely to help the child to grow up according to its own nature, or does education indeed have a more far-reaching aim? At this point there is an immediate clash of opinion between various views of life on the one hand and Christianity on the other.

However, we must proceed carefully in qualifying the views of life. If we confine ourselves to stating that humanism and Christianity clash at this point, then we are bound to go wrong. There are humanistic trends of thought which certainly do accept norms and which indeed regard education as an activity governed by fundamental norms. There are many humanists who look upon pedagogy as a normative science and who state that it is the highest aim of education to inculcate in the child obedience to these norms so that the scope of education is a broader one than merely enabling the child to exercise its inherited talents. Naturally, these humanists find their norms elsewhere than in Christianity, but, strictly speaking, that is not the question which concerns us at this point. Here we are only concerned with the problem of the positive and formal character of pedagogics. It is true that there are certain schools of thought, also humanistic in character, which have declared themselves emphatically in favor of a system of education which virtually denies religious and social norms. There are all sorts of vitalists, irrationalists, national socialists and adherents of the so-called "Lebensphilosophie" who emphatically state that it is the exclusive purpose of education to allow the child to develop in accordance with his nature. Obviously, the doctrine of pragmatism in the United States, the essential character of which is expressed by the statement that the only good education is the one which is useful, and that the only useful thing is for a man to make himself useful in society both to himself and the community, also fails to recognize a normative education in principle.

Therefore it is not surprising that, wherever pragmatism carries much weight, the idea gradually prevails that education is intended exclusively to guide the child in the development of its natural tendencies, and that the thing to do is to remove the obstacles to the effective development of these natural tendencies as much as possible.

When this view is taken, education indeed becomes merely a technique, operating on the knowledge gained from psychology and sociology. In this case there really is no question of a scientific pedagogy. Of course one can philosophize on education and one may speak of a philosophy of education or a pedagogical philosophy, but a scientific pedagogy as an independent science with a closed system is out of the question. This is due to the fact that the concept of education has been defined incorrectly, and so has actually been emptied of its true meaning.

Such a mistaken conception in turn results from the fact that both psychology and sociology have been dissociated from the more fundamental principles of life. The fact is that these two sciences are frequently reduced to the result of exact investigations in the mental and social fields. Though it may be accepted as a general theory that the whole of life is enclosed within principles superior to life, this is not taken into account in one's science. One may be prepared to state that God exists; one may also be willing to say that there is good and evil; one may even acknowledge that the question as to what is good and what evil is determined by a guiding principle given by God or a higher power. Nevertheless, promising as this may seem, it is not sufficient to provide me with a foundation for a scientific pedagogy based on motives of principle. There will always be the risk that in this way my pedagogy continues to be a theory regarding the practical use of psychology and sociology, even though I then add that the human being, concerning whose education I have formulated a theory, must now live in accordance with God's commandment. By proceeding in this manner, one will never obtain a scientific pedagogy. For in that case pedagogy lacks any ideas or conceptions of its own and has no scientific aims of its own. In these instances, all that remains is the application of rules, derived from psychology and sociology.

This becomes entirely different, however, when I am confronted by the question as to how I, by taking into consideration known sociological data and known psychological data regarding the child, must acquaint the child with the religious and moral norms, the norms of truth and beauty. How, I repeat, am I to acquaint the child with these religious and moral norms so as to enable him to grow up in accordance with them, under the discipline of that which I acknowledge to be my principle? If there be a pedagogy that can serve this end, such a pedagogy will indeed have a character and a scientific task of its own. Allow me to explain this by a few examples.

The concept of character is a concept from psychology; the concept of growth of character also is a concept from psychology; but the concept of *formation of character* is a *pedagogical* concept.

Ethics are of importance in the formation of character. But I cannot merely say to the child: "Thou shalt not commit adultery." I must find the pedagogical form for these normative rules. This then is another pedagogical concept: to find the pedagogical forms of the norms. So, too, when I say: "formation of character," I am concerned with the pedagogical concept as such. And I may speak of character formation scientifically only when I also concern myself with that other independent scientific activity, namely, the search for that pedagogical form of the norms which is appropriate to the nature and character of the child and the circumstances under which he is being educated.

This is the process by which a pedagogical science is established. I act on facts which I have derived from psychology and sociology. But as I do so I am a completely independent and scientific individual, engaged in a task, imposed upon me by my subject, that is, *education.* From the nature of this subject it follows that I shall always have to deal with the following factors:

First: the child who has to be educated;
Second: the educator who has the vocation to education;
Third: the object which is aimed at in education; and
Fourth: the method which must be used.

All these points raise questions of a completely individual nature which do not fit in any branch of science and which belong only in pedagogy.

The question as to how I regard *the child from a religious and ethical point of view* is the factor which determines the pedagogical system. If, like Rousseau, I regard children as good by nature, or if, like many moderns, I consider them to be religiously indifferent, this will be reflected in my entire system. And consequently an entirely different system will inevitably follow for him who, in accordance with the Scriptures, views the child as being together with his parents involved in Adam's fall, but also included in the covenant of grace, provided that grace is present. From the very outset these matters confront pedagogy with tasks of a unique character.

This is true also for *the educator.* It is indeed possible to regard parents as educators who are merely related to the child biologically, or as people whose duty to bring up the child stems only from biological ties. But the parent-child relationship will be fundamentally different when the ties between parents and children are primarily regarded as religious in nature. According to the Scriptures, parents are parents in the first place because they sustain the same relationship to God. The duty of the parents arises primarily from a mandate which has its origin in the sovereign good pleasure of God. It is the task of pedagogy to shed scientific light on the nature of this mandate. That task belongs to pedagogy exclusively, although it in turn will frequently derive certain normative rules from other sciences, for example, from theology. The question, however, as to what concrete measures are incumbent on the parents by virtue of their religious relationship to their children, cannot and may not be answered by theology, but must be answered by pedagogy.

Quite obviously, if someone takes a *normative* view different from that of Christianity, as for instance the view of humanism, he will, in thinking out his science, *formally* arrive at a pedagogical structure identical with that which we have here defined.

Again it will be immediately apparent that the question of principle also predominates in determining *the object* aimed at in pedagogy. The question, which can only be answered by *scientific* investigations, is how to formulate the object in accordance with our principle and how to relate this object to both the psychologically possible and to available sociological data. We need hardly state this results in a very special study of *methodology*.

It will be clear, however, that, regardless of the principles held, every pedagogue who wishes to develop a unified system, must arrive at a scientific pedagogy. This no longer is the application of psychology, this is not the transfer of sentences from theology or philosophy to a different field; this is an independent utilization of data from the auxiliary sciences, psychology and sociology, and the independent application of norms from the normative sciences with a view to the task imposed by one's own science, pedagogy.

If anyone should claim, that, owing to all these borrowings from various sciences, it will be impossible for pedagogy to maintain its independence, I should like to reply: First, that today there is not a single science that is able to manage without borrowing from other sciences. Theology takes counsel with Hebrew and Greek philology and literature, with logic and with history; chemistry consults physics and mathematics; medicine cannot possibly manage without physics, biology and chemistry. In the last resort not a single science is completely independent of the others. Second, I should like to challenge my opponent to show me any other science in which specifically pedagogical features are the predominating factor. Education always wishes to change, to call into being that which does not exist; it wants to realize ideals which do not exist as yet by means of concretely available data on the one, and by appropriate measures on the other hand; but all activity is invariably aimed at this changing and this accomplishing of ideals. Hence concepts such as formation of character, formation of personality, and education are highly specific of a science such as pedagogy.

It follows that pedagogy is largely a *theoria ad praxin.* But these practical aims are not its sole aspect. For the seeking of the pedagogical forms of the norms, the determination of the child's moral structures, the definition of the boundaries of the rights and obligations of the parents, and many other similar points are theoretical in nature and all these activities have a specific character.

If anyone should remark that therefore pedagogy is after all a kind of *philosophia minor,* it will be obvious that such a remark suggests a considerable misapprehension. Philosophy can never be a *theoria ad praxin* and philosophy can never be directed towards a concrete act; though philosophy may speak of man in its anthropology, philosophy by its very nature can never speak of the significance of man's God-given mandate to attain a certain end with his children, nor of the concrete formulation of that object in the instance of a particular child.

Accordingly, we have arrived at the conclusion that he who regards the character of education as *an acting according to norms,* must inevitably acknowledge that pedagogy is an independent science.

But now we are also able to understand that the principle upon which we base our education will decide the character of our scientific pedagogy. If anything, the relationship between education and pedagogy will indeed show to what extent life is a unity and how little sense there is in separating theory from practice.

Thus we can answer the question as to what are the foundations of Christian pedagogy. Here we must again make a preliminary remark, however. In every science, especially a science so in the center of living practice as pedagogy, we should hold on to the thought that nearly all vital phenomena contribute to the construction of a scientific totality. And in dealing with the foundations of such a science, we must not forget that this science is concerned with a subject matter obtained from other sciences. These other sciences also have their foundations. In citing certain statements from theology we must not forget, for example, that theological views in turn are also based on certain foundations. The insight into the inspiration of the Scriptures is typical of the result obtained by theology. And we could go on in this manner.

From the foregoing we draw two implications. In the first place, it is out of the question to include all principles with which pedagogy comes into contact among the foundations of scientific pedagogy. A detailed theory of organic inspiration belongs to dogmatics, not to pedagogy. Pedagogy simply accepts the findings of dogmatics. This implies a considerable limitation in describing the foundations of pedagogy. The foundations of pedagogy should be provided by the bases of its own structure. In Amsterdam houses are built on piles. These piles are obtained from a forest, which possibly grows in Sweden or Switzerland. But these piles are ready for use when they arrive at the building site and the architect is not concerned with the structure of these piles, the structure of their cells, and the history of all the years in which the trees were growing. He will accept these piles as means of support. He will ask only: are these piles usable? And upon these piles he will build the foundations of his house.

It is the same in science and in pedagogy. Therefore we should here attempt to ascertain the nature of our own pedagogical foundations of pedagogical science.

At the very outset, however, we must make one further observation. If we accept a certain material prior to building our pedagogical house, this material should fit into the system which we devise. It must be usable for our house. This means that if we wish to build a Christian pedagogy, we cannot borrow any fundamental tenets from humanistic philosophy or liberal theology. For the fundamental tenets, even those of the great among our colleagues who hold views based on different principles, do not fit into the structure we are building. He who intends to speak of Christian discipline cannot borrow certain fundamental tenets regarding the nature of parental authority from a book written by a radical jurist, or rather, he may do so, but in that event he is doing something that is not scientifically justified. For the ideas which he borrows from that book are at variance with the meaning of the system which he is attempting to build. It follows that there must always be harmony between the principles of the fundamental and auxiliary sciences on the one hand, and between these and pedagogy on the other hand.

Just now I have defined the auxiliary and normative sciences as two different groups. In doing this, I regard auxiliary sciences as those sciences from which we may borrow any material we may require. These auxiliary sciences are psychology and sociology. These sciences cannot compel pedagogy to adopt particular data. Pedagogy merely accepts their help, in so far as it has need of it.

The case is different with regard to the fundamental—or normative — sciences. They lay down the norms to which pedagogy has to adjust itself. Pedagogy, however, accepts full responsibility for incorporating these norms in such a way that they take on a particular form in the pedagogical system.

I sense that an objection will be raised at this point. Someone will remark that in this way I tend to build a pedagogical system which is completely isolated in life, in that it makes for a Christian pedagogy and a Christian education which are more or less antagonistic to all sorts of non-Christian systems and which have no use for anything from non-Christian systems.

Here we touch on a point about which there is considerable misconception. But this misconception exists only for those who do not completely understand the situation. Naturally, even if it were true that Christian pedagogy were in such a position that scientific material could be obtained only from fellow Christians, I would still have to accept this situation. For indeed, Christians are not afraid of being isolated. At Golgotha there also was a small group which said "yes" to the cross, whereas the majority cried "no" to the Lord of the universe.

Yet the pattern is not a simple one of black and white, as might initially be imagined. This is indeed the case when we are dealing with normative sciences; in that event it is a matter of accepting or rejecting the Word of God. But the situation is entirely different with regard to those sciences which offer us all sorts of material: psychology and sociology. In this case we must indeed also be extremely careful. For someone's view, based on principle, may all too readily affect the results which he obtains. We must be sure that, in borrowing the findings of a psychologist or sociologist, we do not after all swallow a principle which we have rejected.

Nevertheless, owing to God's common grace, people still possess so much common sense that they are able to identify all kinds of data, particularly concerning the facts of daily life, which are correct and which they are able to describe correctly, regardless of the views which they hold. As soon as activities assume a more or less technical character, the conclusions drawn by Christians and non-Christians will frequently be identical. As a result people of all sorts of opinions are able to live together. When the temperatures in the house of a Christian and a non-Christian are identical, the thermometer will indicate an equal number of degrees; a stone will fall down perpendicularly both in the garden of a Christian and in that of a heathen; and an appendectomy is performed by a Christian physician and a non-Christian physician in the same hospital according to an identical procedure.

Accordingly, there need be no fear of a complete isolation of Christian pedagogy. The child's process of development, its use of conceptions and concepts, the degree to which it is capable of abreaction of neurotic tensions in the playroom, its response to unjust discipline, and a variety of other things are identical, regardless of the system of education employed. Two people, driving down the same road, the one to a brothel and the other to church, use the same road surface, breathe the same kind of air and see the same trees and houses along the road. But their *heart* is different and subsequently at a certain moment their paths will diverge. But they also come from different houses and they also hold different views and essentially they are also doing something different in driving along that road. In social intercourse, however, they are not isolated from each other. This may also be our view with regard to pedagogy.

Bearing in mind what we have said above, we may now seek to establish the foundations of Christian pedagogy.

One of the first questions confronting pedagogy is the question as to the character and nature of children. We have deliberately formulated this in a general way and have not qualified character and nature by an adjectival modifier. For we indeed mean that the character and nature of children in every relationship are concerned, that is, the child's character and nature in the religious sense, the ethical sense, the emotional sense, and the like.

The question of our position with regard to children will of course be determined predominantly by our view of man as defined in our basic principles. And, as we have stated previously and will frequently repeat later on: in the first place we consider man to be a creature of God, created after God's image and therefore a religious entity. This is far more significant than if we merely say: we view the child as created by God and as a sinful child requiring regeneration. Man is a rational and moral being; but he is so merely because he is a religious being. Accordingly, the rational and moral features do not constitute two aspects of existence, which are separately governed like independent provinces, but they are two organically interlocking aspects of existence, which may both be attributed to the fact that man is religious. This "being religious" has a very broad sense. It means much more than that man should fear God in his life. That too. But it also means that man can and should live human life in its fullest sense. All his specifically human relationships result from the fact that man is religious. Emotional attachments, ambitions, evaluations, social attachments—in short, all that which is humanly sublime in the life of man exists only because man is the offspring of God. Thus one may say that in the marriage bond, in the ties between parents and their children, in true friendship, in commiseration with social distress, there is something of the religious which causes man to be man.

Regarding the character and nature of this religious being of man, we accept the Holy Scriptures, the Word of God, as the source by which truth may be known. It is from this source that we receive light on the nature and significance of man as a religious entity.

Thus we also know that man has been created towards God and that in his inner self, at the inmost core of his existence, there is a religious bond with God. Whatever this core may be called, whether it is called "heart" (with reference, incorrectly in my opinion, to the Scriptures), "religious root" or, as I believe to be more correct, the "self" proper, is immaterial. We here prefer to use the term "the self of man." The Bible warrants such a use.

Now the essential characteristic of this "self" of man is that it is religious, that is, that it has been created with a view to service. Religion is more than a mere *Abhängigkeitsgefühl* (feeling of dependence). Religion is being active in submission to Him whom one adores and worships; being active in the service of the adored. Now this service, this devotion to Him, to whom we have surrendered ourselves because He has conquered us, manifests itself in the threefold aspect of man's existence. It manifests itself, first, in and through man's cognitive approach to God himself and to God in all his works. and therefore also in his creation; second, it manifests itself in the surrender, in the dedication to God and his works in all the cosmos, which He has created; and third, it manifests itself in the wish to reign and plan in this cosmos in the service of God. Accordingly, the fact that man is religious presents three aspects: that of knowledge, that of surrender, and that of rule. These three aspects, according to the Scriptures, are those of the three offices of prophet, priest and king.

Now we also know from the Scriptures that man has fallen away from God. This fall means that his "self" has taken a different direction. The "self" of man did retain the image of God in a broader sense, so that it has preserved the need to serve and it has also preserved the need to serve in the three aspects, the three offices. However, since this service has taken a different direction, man by nature no longer serves God, but virtually serves creatures, preferably himself. Thus the *object* of man's life has shifted completely. Man thus becomes a prophet, priest and king in the service of his own self; and self-glorification becomes the ultimate goal of his existence. Ego-centrism and subsequently egoism becomes the trend of all his moral actions. And even when man succeeds in freeing himself, at least of *conscious* self-glorification, he will get no further than serving the creatures by which he is surrounded. According to the Scriptures one of the fundamental characteristics of sin is to *miss* the purpose of life. Accordingly, sin is not a quantitative thing and, we might even state, it is not a qualitative thing in the positive sense. Sin does not impart a particular quality, it merely deprives of a particular quality. Owing to sin we miss our object, and our need to serve in the religious sense—which perforce is present in the self—is aimed at the wrong object.

The grace which enters into life—that is the significance, the meaning of the coming of Christ in human flesh. And the significance, the meaning of the Word, is that God has seen fit to find a way by which life may be restored, so that man may find God again as the One whom he serves, as the One toward whom his religious existence was aimed originally. This implies three things: In the *first* place it implies a merciful disposition on the part of God to pardon the blame which man has incurred by turning away from Him. In the *second* place it implies a work of God in man, by which the inner man is transformed, so that in principle the object of his service no longer is the creature, but again becomes the Creator. And in the *third* place it implies guidance by God's Spirit, which enables man to die to the attitude of creature-glorification, that he may learn to live increasingly in sanctification according to the will of God. Viewed objectively, this forgiveness of sin is the reckoning of the righteousness, which Christ has acquired, by God to man, who receives grace in regeneration and justification.

The transformation of man is a fruit of regeneration, which is worked by the Spirit of God in the heart of man and which manifests itself in conversion, which implies a change in mind on the one hand, and a change in walk of life on the other hand. Regeneration enables man to accept salvation in Christ, because God works that faith in the heart of man by regeneration. This faith is not a new creation. Natural man also believes. But he directs his faith toward things other than God. The man who lives by the faith which God has given him will direct his faith toward God's promises and toward God's grace in Christ; he will also direct that faith toward the obedience which he owes God by virtue of the fact that God has the right to command obedience and because God is God and therefore his Lord and Master.

The foundations of Christian pedagogy are of course also concerned with the educator. One can only be an educator when charged with this mission. "To be an educator" always implies a particular legal relationship with the individual to be educated. This relationship to the young person who is to be educated does not primarily result from a voluntary decision made by the educator. In some cases this voluntary decision may be required in the second instance. But invariably the educator will be one who is entitled to be an educator by virtue of the fact that he has been charged with a mission. "To be an educator" always bears the character of carrying out an official mission.

Accordingly, education also includes an element of responsibility. This responsibility, however, can only be realized in the way of love. But we hope to discuss this in detail in our third lecture.

And here we have to draw attention to a problem which plays an extremely important part in Christian pedagogy. The danger is not imaginary that we sometimes wish to solve the problems arising in the various areas of life's relationships directly from our religious starting-point. In doing so, we but too readily forget that this solution frequently is an activity of logical thought, rather than of our faith and religious function.

If we wish to see education take its correct place in the relationships of life and if we wish to form a correct idea of educational practice, we shall indeed have to resist any dualism in our starting-point on the one hand, but on the other hand we shall also consistently have to take the view that duality is an acknowledged fact. *Duality,* not as though there were an eternal conflict in the *dualistic* sense between two principles which are mutually exclusive, but rather in the sense that we understand that we can reflect believingly on the truth regarding life and God's relation to life according to his revelation only if we see the two-sidedness inherent in the whole of life and every relationship of life.

This immediately concerns our relationship with and our knowledge of God. God is transcendent and immanent. He is the sovereign Lord of all creatures and independently of every creature he worketh all things after the counsel of his will. But God is also immanent. We are in him, but he also is in every creature. Indeed, we can never conceive this immanence and this transcendence as a unity. We may believingly accept that these two are united in God and in his relationship to the creature, but we can only experience this truth concerning God as duality—once again, this is something else than dualism. Therefore unity can be found only in the religious starting-point; in the acknowledgement of the fact that we are there to serve God and that we also have to subject ourselves to God in our thinking. We must know and accept this duality not only with regard to the revelation which God has given us concerning himself, but also in other respects.

We wish now to draw attention to some aspects of this duality which also are of particular importance in education. He who accepts God's ordinance of life and believes that God works all things after his counsel and his ordinance according to an eternal plan, but simultaneously accepts the full responsibility of man and the causal relationship governing his actions, must acknowledge that he accepts those two side by side, but that he can never think of them as united. To be sure, in faith we may avow that they are united in God and we may formulate terms such as these: that God has also included our talents and our responsibility in his counsel, but we can never intellectually comprehend the nature of this relationship between God's counsel and our responsibility.

Another example: inducement to repentance also has a place of its own in education. Now the Scriptures tell us on the one hand that man must repent; "repent ye" is a recurrent exhortation of the Scriptures. But on the other hand it is equally true, that God *gives* repentance. Repentance is inconceivable without regeneration and the Scriptures themselves tell us that God gives Israel repentance and remission of sins. The prayer: "Turn thou us unto thee, O Lord, and we shall be turned," points in the same direction. Here again we arrive at the duality of our mission in the work of God—a duality that we may not accentuate into a twofold principle such as dualism, but which, on the other hand, we can also never rationally conceive as a unity.

It is impossible for man to think simultaneously in the one and in the other category. This applies to every relationship of life. For the duality of which we spoke does not obtain merely in the religious sphere. The relationship of love between man and wife is characterized by a permanent tension between cause and effect on the one hand, and between ends and means on the other. Loving because one is loved, and loving in order that one may show the partner one's love, and again receive love, may be comprised within a single loving activity. But we cannot rationally think of these two as one.

Here we are confronted with the problem, universally admitted in philosophy, of the relationship between the causal and the final or teleological. The law of cause and effect and the law of object and effective use of the causal means aimed at an end, are by no means mutually exclusive. In the practice of daily life we intuitively experience the unity of these two. But it will be impossible for us to think *rationally* of these two as a unity, if at least by thinking we wish to obtain more than a dead formula with which we seem to state something, but with which we really do nothing else than find a sanctuary for our lack of insight.

In the practice of pedagogy we shall therefore continually come up against the fact of duality. One may try to get away from this fact of duality by saying that it is not a true duality, since the relationships continue to present themselves in a different connection. One may draw attention to the fact that, for example, in the problem of God's counsel and our responsibility things may, in the one case, be regarded as being within the sphere governed by the laws laid down by God himself unto himself with respect to his own creative acts and his own foresight concerning creation; and in another case, the same event may be viewed within the sphere of our own actions toward our fellow-men, toward ourselves or toward God. But none of these arguments solves the difficulty, by any means. At most they will explain why we always see things as a duality. But even possessing this explanation, no one can imagine and think of these two, God's counsel and our responsibility, as a unity. Indeed, the Bible itself very accurately defines this duality in a text like the following: "Work out your own salvation with fear and trembling; for it is God which worketh in you both to will and to work, for his good pleasure" (Phil. 2:12-13).

The acceptance of this *duality* entails extremely important consequences upon pedagogy from the point of view of principle. To begin with, there is a point to education only when God uses this education as a method to bring the child where he wishes him to be. Ultimately any use of methods will only yield results when God blesses these methods. This implies that education should always occur in dependence on God. But this also means that nothing is to be subtracted from the absolute demand made by God that parents shall educate their children and that one day the parents shall have to give an account of this education. And it is not merely in this field that duality is operative. This law of the twofold aspect of life operates throughout education.

The educator must lead the child to the goal which he proposes in accordance with the norms which he has adopted. And at the same time the educator must develop that which is present in the child, for he cannot introduce what God has not placed in the child. Development and formation, growth and education, inner entelechy and being directed toward an end as an object—these invariably are two aspects which should be a real unity in educational practice. Not such a unity, I repeat, that they may also be *conceived* as a unity. Once more, to our thinking they will at best always represent *two* aspects of a *single* matter. But it should be so that man *experiences* the unity of his actions and God's work *as a unity in faith.* And in educating the child in wisdom according to those forms of the norms which are particularly adapted to the child in view of the child's age and nature, he should accept the unity of ability and goal in a faithful optimism as to what God will allow this child to grow into.

Although to our thinking duality always actually exists and although only faith is able to comply with the demand to accept this duality as a unity, we have not thereby reached the end of our considerations.

God as the Creator of all that lives is One. Likewise his creatures are one. The Scriptures more than once stress the unity of creation far more consistently than we as a rule observe it in daily life. Probably we should not dare to say that the whole creation waiteth with earnest expectation for the day that the glory of the children of God shall be revealed (Rom. 8), if it did not say so in the Bible. The fact that plants and trees, insects and fishes, are looking forward to the *parousia,* in earnest expectation at that, be it that this expectation is not a conscious act, suggests a unity of the whole creation that we may not disregard. Hence we must teach our children a regard for life not only, but we must also view their life as being wonderfully in harmony and at one with all that buds, grows, blossoms, bears fruit, and dies around us. The law of life applies to everything that lives; this is also true of the law of death. And if the educators were merely engaged in helping children to pass through the process of maturation preliminary to death as elegantly as possible, they would be faced with a tremendous task. The education of children would be an anxious and hopeless work. But the meaning of life is not death; we can only understand the meaning of life, if in this life we know ourselves to be bound to him who is the Creator and who creates life only so that one day life may be triumphant.

Hence we can detach neither life nor education from Jesus Christ. Through him and in him people are not only prepared for a new heaven and a new earth, but the whole creation, purified and glorified, shall one day live to the glory of God. The object of the work of education is not to manage the parade for death, but rather the organization, with Christ, of the victory over death and the grave. This is indicated by our form for baptism: "And when we are baptized in the name of the Son, the Son seals unto us that he washes us in his blood from all our sins, incorporating us into the fellowship of his death and resurrection."

Thus we see that, from the very outset, education means establishing the relationship between the lives of children and Jesus Christ. And this not only in the sense of "acquainting these children with the salvation of redemption from their sins." That also. But Christian education cannot even isolate from the totality of life this bringing of Christ as Savior, for Christ does not deliver part of man merely, nor part of creation merely, but he delivers the whole of human life and the whole of creation. Accordingly, redemption in Christ encompasses the whole of life and all relationships of life; so that in this sense it is completely universal.

That this does not mean that every man participates in redemption need not be emphasized here. It remains true that the tree of God's planting will be redeemed, but that those who by their own fault will be dry branches shall wither from the bough and not commune with the root.

From this something more follows as well. If Christ governs the whole of life, there cannot even be an inner contradiction in that life. When contradiction appears to manifest itself, this is primarily due to the rule of sin in creation; consequently, this results from the fact that there are tendencies in the fallen world which resist Christ and God. This also explains how Paul, in Romans 7, can complain of the sin which still dwells in him. In this life sanctification is merely partial and incomplete, so that it is an unceasing process. But in principle life is under the dominion of Christ, so that Paul is able to say: "So it is no more I that do it, but sin which dwelleth in me."

As a result of this unity of life, there can be *no breach* between the various spheres of life. Someone may say, "This man or that industry will benefit *socially,* but will be harmed from an *economic* point of view if a certain measure is taken." But without a doubt that statement is incorrect, at least if we consider more than just the immediate results of the deed or act which we observe. Essentially social and economic events are closely related. To assume a contradiction between these spheres in the sense that something by which life benefits socially might be harmful from an economic point of view, would lead to the acceptance of a complete division of life into spheres incompatible with one another.

And this does not only apply to the general sphere of life; it applies also to the life of the individual. At this point we enter an area which may be of fundamental importance in the practice of education. There are educators who believe that a child may benefit by certain measures from an intellectual point of view; but then they will sometimes conclude that this measure is not conducive to the formation of character in that child. For example, a child which has difficulty in learning, which is constantly being hounded with private lessons and always being urged to earn better grades, will become peevish, surly, tiresome and later perhaps untrustworthy. The remark then made by certain educators, that what is essential to the intellectual education of the child apparently is detrimental to his character formation, is incorrect. He who regards this child as a manifestation of an individual life which is a unity in itself should understand that those things which this child cannot bear, cannot stand, cannot cope with because of the limited character of his intellectual faculties, will naturally also spoil the child's character. This is not due to physical influences, but to the fact that the demands made upon this child disturb its emotional life, interfere with its inner life, destroy its courage, mar its moral sense, and imperil the whole of its character; for all this learning is not suited to this child.

It is *this unity of life* which we are continually able to observe and which we are able to experience with joy, time and again. Consequently, to him who has regard for life and the laws of life as instituted by God, the experience in daily life of the dualities, as described previously, will only be a reality when he approaches the problems solely from an intellectual point of view. A rational approach to the problems must lead us to the recognition of duality. Therefore a purely scientific analysis of the problems will always confront us with these dualities.

But he who lives by faith cannot express himself only in the acceptance of the unity of all God's work in faith; in the practice of daily life he will also—if he simply accepts life, as God has placed it before him—find little or no occasion to take offence at the poignancy of any duality.

And thus we naturally come to the conclusion that there is a *danger* to life itself in a *one-sided rational* approach. The human intellect, which disects everything, analyzes everything, counts everything and measures everything, is itself a product of a life-dissolving activity. Therefore any science and any pedagogy which arises merely from this isolated *ratio,* is doomed to death; for though the man who tells you exactly how many sepals, and petals, how many stamens and what pistil he has picked from the flower you gave him may speak very accurately and very scientifically, he is not speaking of the *flower* which God has caused to grow. For in nature, stamens and pistils, petals and sepals do not grow: God has made *flowers.*

And he who understands this, who is able to attain the harmony between head and heart, who learns to know with his heart and to love with his intellect—and this is the knowing and loving repeatedly mentioned in the Scriptures—he will also experience the unity of life in education. He will not today be engaged in religious education and tomorrow in intellectual education, nor will he be occupied now in morally educating the child, and then in esthetically training him. He will understand that life is one, and that both in himself, the educator, and in the child which he is educating, this one life must express itself and develop according to the rule given by the Creator, in order that he may be, and the child may become, a man of God.

2

The Objective of Christian Education

ONE of the most important questions in education is: What do we really want to achieve through the process of education? The concern of education is ever the establishment of an ideal, the positing of a goal or objective. The educator who lacks an objective cannot educate.

As I stated in my first lecture, some modern pedagogues claim that education is nothing more than furnishing a child with the opportunity to develop according to his own nature. Education, it is said, has a two-fold task: negatively, it must seek to remove the obstacles to self-development; positively, it must make the conditions for this development as favorable as possible. The process of self-development, of course, includes the adjustment of the individual to the community.

Actually, this manner of determining the goal of education is based upon a conviction. Of course, the educator who defines education in this way believes that we must discover the essential nature of the child first of all in the totality of his inherited traits, and secondly in his future adult role in society. With respect to the moral and religious nature of the child, these educators make no commitment and assume no responsibility. The validity of this non-committal position has not been scientifically established. The position develops, rather, from a definite life and world view which is pre-scientific in character. And thus, to a certain extent, the position is based upon a religious conviction.

It is necessary that we who take a confessional point of view should understand this well. In many scientific circles there is a tendency to regard a position of religious indifferentism as being more scientific than one of religious commitment. It is argued that if you begin with a certain religious conviction and take a definite religious viewpoint, you limit yourself scientifically and consequently you are no longer free in your scientific judgment. This point of view is based on a very serious misconception. As a matter of fact, without a pre-scientific commitment, no science is possible. Even the natural sciences are based upon the so-called "pre-scientific insight." In the final analysis the meaning and the content of concepts such as warmth, speed, value, judgment and the like, are derived from non-scientific life. Our argument becomes even more cogent when we begin the real scientific task: the explanation of relationships. This type of scientific work requires a life and world view based on principles. Without this vision we simply cannot begin the scientific task. Let us not forget that the man who makes a simple experiment and proceeds on the assumption that it is possible that the observed results are accurate and verifiable by others, has started out by assuming a considerable pre-scientific life and world view. There are educators who determine the nature of education on the basis of the assumption that the child must be regarded both as an individual and as a social creature. They regard religion and morality as a matter of subsequent conviction, and hence of no concern to the educator. These educators, I say, have made a judgment regarding the nature of religion and morality which is not at all scientifically established, but which proceeds simply from their basic convictions.

Therefore, it follows that these basic convictions must be taken into account in positing objectives for education; it is in fact the basis from which one proceeds. This is as true for a nihilist, a pragmatist, a fundamentalist, as it is for a communist. And each time we discover anew that this point of view is a matter of personal belief, which, seen from a particular perspective, may be designated as unbelief.

If this is true, we can proceed to establish a second fact—the fact, namely, that the entire educational process is governed by objectives. What end do we seek for the child? The answer to that question determines all our activity.

But at the outset it should be clearly understood that the formulation of educational objectives is no simple matter. Allow me to illustrate. At a beach along the North Sea in the Netherlands some time ago, I saw a child with a paper bag. The child had the bag for a purpose. His little friend had caught a small fish. The little boy now wanted to put water into the bag so that the fish could swim in it. Then he wanted to take the fish to his mother who was sitting on a hotel terrace some distance away. Accordingly, the bag was filled with sea water and the fish was put into it. With the bag full of water in his hand, the little fellow ran to his mother. But before he had come half way the bag was soaked through. Suddenly it burst and both water and fish were spilled on the beach. In setting up his objective, the child had not taken into account the nature of the paper bag.

By this illustration I merely wish to indicate that in setting up goals for education we must begin by possessing a very considerable knowledge of the nature and potentialities of the child. And a scientifically adequate statement of the aims of education can be formulated neither by psychology nor theology, but only by the science of pedagogy.

This is true not only because pedagogical science alone can make judgments concerning the nature of the child and its pedagogical potentialities, but also for two additional reasons. In the first place, pedagogy as a science is alone qualified to judge the significance of the influence which the educator and the entire environment can exert upon the child. In the second place, the science of pedagogy alone is able to formulate religious and moral ideals which are appropriate to, and can become active in, the life of the child so that presently he accepts social norms and becomes religiously mature.

Once this is understood, it becomes evident that the definition of educational objectives is not a simple task. Not only must we carefully take into consideration concrete situations, but we must also possess a thorough insight into the total structure of principles involved.

The question: How are we to define the aims of education? has been answered in very different ways. The attempts of Christian educators to describe the goal of education in conformity with various statements of the Holy Scriptures are striking. Herman Bavinck's definition, based on 2 Timothy 3: 17, seems to me to be the most successful of these attempts. He says: "The child must be formed to become 'the man of God, furnished completely unto every good work.' " There is something very appealing about formulating the goal of education in this manner. After all, you are employing a scriptural term; a dispute about terminology is only remotely possible. In such a formulation everyone has in mind the meaning of the text in question.

However, the question remains whether the method of employing a specific text for a very special purpose is justifiable. Indeed, it must be self-evident that the original text in question was not written *for the purpose of defining the goal of education.* Let us examine more carefully the example provided by Bavinck's definition. Obviously, the text of 2 Timothy 3: 17 deals only in a very indirect way with the problem of education. In the immediately preceding verse we read: "Every Scripture inspired of God is also profitable for teaching, for reproof, for correction, for instruction which is in righteousness." And the following verse concludes: "that the man of God may be complete, furnished unto every good work." The thrust of these verses is a declaration that the Holy Scriptures by virtue of their divine inspiration are profitable to the man of God in four respects. That is to say, they gradually bring about in men who are filled with the Spirit of God a condition in which they listen obediently, a condition in which they are "equal" to the claims of God. Actually, this text makes a declaration concerning the Holy Scriptures. And in connection with this declaration about Holy Writ, it is stated further that the purpose of Scripture is also the perfecting of the man of God. Obviously, it is difficult to take this same text as a statement of the purpose of education in general.

Another observation must be made. It is very evident that Paul in this text refers not only to those who are to be educated, but also to those who must do the educating. Taken in its context, the reference is to the forming of office-bearers through the Holy Scriptures. The persons to whom reference is made are not only the pupils, but also the teachers; not only the children but also the parents. Besides, we must observe that the contextual reference is to the importance of the work of office-bearers in the church. Indeed, after 2 Timothy 3: 17, we read: "I charge thee in the sight of God, and of Jesus Christ: . . . Preach the word, be urgent in season, out of season; reprove, rebuke, exhort, with all longsuffering and teaching. . . ." The entire context, therefore, clearly refers to the labors of officebearers in the midst of the congregation.

However good the definition of Herman Bavinck appears to be, it raises so many questions that we should not, in my judgment, follow in his footsteps.

Is it then not correct to say that the goal of education should be to form the child into the man of God? Certainly, that is correct. But we must not overlook the fact that in deriving our definition from a particular Bible text, we thereby give a specific meaning to our definition. By formulating our definition in the terms of a given text of the Bible, the definition inevitably takes on the specific meaning of that text. Indeed, in general we should disapprove the practice of using a text which refers only indirectly to education and interpret its meaning so that it refers primarily and exclusively to education.

However, two important questions then remain to be answered. First: Is there any Bible text which we can use to define the goal of education? Second: If we cannot find such a text in the Bible, is it nevertheless possible in general to define the aim of education in a single statement?

In my judgment, the first question must be answered negatively. To be sure, we can read many things in the Bible about education in general; but if we look for a definition of education in all of its aspects, we will not find it there. We do find all kinds of descriptions of good education, including such as: "teaching in the fear of the Lord," and "training up a young man in the way he should go," and so on. But it should be clear that none of these gives a definition of education in the broadest sense.

In addition to this we must observe that a definition of the objective of education should have the characteristics of a scientific statement. If we are to write a book on pedagogy, the definition of educational objectives should be in scientifically acceptable terminology: that is, our definition must be appropriate to a scientific discussion. The comprehensive character of such a description should characterize it as a definitive statement, a *definition*. Furthermore, in such a definitive statement, we shall have to take into account the progress of science.

From the foregoing observations it is evident that we shall not find in the Bible a statement of the objectives of education such as is required for pedagogics. The Bible is not a handbook for science. And, besides, from what has been said it follows that the definition of educational objectives is always more or less subject to changes in our temporal order. It is quite possible that a given social or cultural structure will influence the manner in which I define that goal. This also implies that the definition of educational goals may properly reflect changing circumstances. A primitive native Christian in Nigeria or

Malaya will define the goal of education for his people differently than a Dutchman or an American in 1954. If, however, we choose a Bible text for our definition, then it is inconceivable that we can do justice to this variable element in the aim of education. Hence, I submit that no Bible text can furnish us with a scientifically adequate definition of the objective of education.

Of course I do not mean to suggest that in formulating a definition we shall not be bound to take into consideration all that the Scriptures have to say on our subject. On the contrary, we are duty-bound to incorporate every Scriptural statement on the purpose of education into our definition.

We should keep in mind, however, that our account of the aims of education must be in fact a general definition. On the one hand, it must be a general definition incorporating the system of principles supporting the educational goal; and on the other hand, it must reflect the temporal character of education to which we referred, while yet possessing general validity.

The purpose of education, taken in a general sense, resides in the individual himself. Not exclusively in the individual, as we shall note presently, but certainly in the first instance in the individual. *This* child must become an adult who takes care of, and disciplines, himself, who has learned to adjust himself to his social environment, and who, quite as well, knows and fulfills his task and calling in life in every area to which God calls him.

So it becomes evident that the goal of education is also related to the social structures of life. The end of the education of the individual includes the church. But the individual is also educated with a view to the state—in fact, with a view to every social relationship which he sustains. One could even say that his education has an economic aspect. Furthermore, education has historical relevance. The child to be educated, must, as an adult, affiliate himself with history in his own way and he must be able to make history. In short, the sum total of life's relationships is involved in the education of the individual man; but then we must also conclude that implicit in each of these relationships is an aspect of the goal of education.

But precisely because education has bearing on all of life's relationships, it must reflect something of the nature of these relationships. For example, if we say that among other aims, education has a national end, then our definition of the goal of education will also have to take into account, and will be determined by, the structure of that national life.

In the light of these considerations, we can now attempt to answer the question whether or not it is possible to delimit the goal of education in a single statement. There is something appealing about formulating a single sentence to express the educational objective. However, a single-sentence description, necessarily limited in scope, has, in addition to many advantages, also a disadvantage. The disadvantage is that it readily leads to misunderstanding since the number of limiting conditions, being so restricted, makes impossible the understanding or explanation of a larger number of relevant factors.

To the question: Can the goal of education be defined in a single statement? I am inclined to answer as follows. Indeed, it is possible to do so; but surely it is not desirable to limit oneself too narrowly to such a statement in a more extended discussion of the educational objective.

If I were asked to give a single-sentence statement of the aim of education, I should prefer to formulate the definition as follows:

The forming of man into an independent personality serving God according to his Word, able and willing to employ all his God-given talents to the honor of God and for the well-being of his fellow-creatures, in every area of life in which man is placed by God.

As far as the principles are concerned, I regard the positing of this definition of the goal of education as justifiable. But I hasten to remark that there are several difficulties in this definition.

To define education as the forming of an "independent personality who serves God according to his Word," of necessity involves the use of several concepts which can be questioned. "Independent personality" can be interpreted so that it conflicts with "serving God according to his Word." Indeed, even the concept "personality" really demands further elucidation. When we speak of "personality" we think of a personality in which integration and discipline have been satisfactorily achieved. This we express by the single phrase: "independent personality." But by "independent personality" we can also mean a person who, from a social point of view, is able to provide for his own needs. Furthermore, the concept "independent personality" may be used to designate an individual in whom integration has not taken place, or has taken place to a partial degree. However, if we were to give an extended description of the word "personality" in our definition, our statement would become too long and therefore too difficult to use as a definition.

Similar observations could be made concerning the second part of our definition. "Able and willing" includes all kinds of qualities of personality and character. But the question might be raised whether this "ability" refers to the structure of character or has reference to the religious and moral essence of the personality. Besides, one could ask in how far this "able and willing" can or may be taken in an absolute sense. Indeed, no one "is perfectly able to perform his task" and in this imperfect world "willingness" is often a relative matter.

Everyone will feel that all the limitations inherent in a concise description also apply to our definition. However, it may be necessary, for didactic reasons, to make such a concise definition. To what extent that is laudable, it is difficult to say, but it remains a fact that in their examinations professors reveal a distinct preference for definitions. Well, in such an instance the definition we have given may be of service. One should keep in mind, however, that the terminology of the definition must be interpreted in conformity with the totality of my conceptions.

In treating more extensively of the problems of the aims of education, we find a number of key ideas in the definition. First of all, the aim of education is directed towards *forming* the individual: that is, the realization of the potentialities with which God has endowed this particular child, his creature. In the process of education, therefore, it is necessary always to keep in mind that the objective we seek to attain in *this* child must be subordinated to that which is previously present in *this child*.

But this may never mean that we regard as normative the concrete ethical givens in this child. The norm towards which we must direct our goal is always determined by what God tells us in his Word concerning the end of the life of man. Thus our first objective always remains: That man may be the creature of God who serves and honors God with all his talents.

The expression that education is directed *first of all* towards forming the child should not be misunderstood. For it might be concluded that in practice we set up two objectives. First: "We must serve God and be his children." Second: "We must also develop our gifts and talents." Of course, we do not mean that. The meaning is rather: We, as we are, shall honor God with our gifts and talents and all that we possess. Now if there appears to be a conflict between our native capacity and the claim of God, then the claim of God must govern our lives. Nevertheless, such conflict can be explained only in terms of a faulty attitude, a wrong disposition with respect to the problematic nature of life about us and in us.

The demand "to serve God and to honor him with our talents," can be realized only in a well integrated and well regulated personality. By integration is meant the harmonious organization and limitation of the individual's various native capacities and psychical resources with respect to the external world. The entire content of our psychical being: the imagination, percepts and concepts, emotions, feelings, basic drives, desires, wishes, aspirations—in short, our psychic self must be ordered in a harmonious manner so that the result is an equilibrium of the distinct "life structures." In addition it is necessary for the "ego" of the individual to rule this world of the psychical self. Not the psychical, but the spiritual is dominant in human life. This arrangement is a regulative function in which the *regula* of life are to be derived from the law and ordinance of God.

Thus the aim of education is indeed concerned with the forming of this integrated and regulated personality. Anything which can lead to a one-sided emphasis of personal psychical characteristics such as the passions, sentiments, and the like, must be avoided. We must form the child into a harmoniously integrated personality. And above all, this child will have to learn to maintain the order of its personal existence by means of an "ego" which is subject to the ordinances of God.

Once again we observe the goal of educational forming to be simultaneously the fostering of obedient submission to the Word of God and the development of a strong, individual, harmoniously regulated personality.

These two objectives are not in conflict with each other. On the contrary, the one is the condition of the other. This individual is to be so formed as to be a unique person revealing a complete adjustment in all of life's relationships. That requires a balanced character development. But the condition of being "willing and able" to participate in all of life's relationships is not as favorable as one might think at first. Although it is difficult to regard the distinction according to types, as propagated by Spranger and extended by Kerschensteiner, to be valid under all circumstances, it remains true that the one individual tends to develop in one direction, and the other in another direction. It is a simple fact that some individuals are best fitted for political life; that others are better suited for economic affairs; and still others find themselves best in the social sphere. Naturally, this must not to be taken to mean that those "who go into politics" are most suited to carry on politics, nor does it mean that every merchant is a successful businessman. But it does mean that there are different people who have special abilities in one direction or another.

* * *

We must now answer the question whether or not it is the duty of a Christian to be "willing and able" to be actively engaged in every sphere of life. As far as "ability" or "fitness" is concerned, it must be readily admitted that we certainly cannot speak of an explicit requirement. According to the Scriptures God bestows upon one individual this talent, and upon the other that talent. Some individuals simply do not possess native capacities in certain areas of life. And usually there is a certain inner relationship between the extent of a person's qualifications and the degree of his willingness to lend his efforts towards a specific goal.

Consequently, the crux of the matter of being "willing and able" to be active in any sphere of life must not be sought in a "willingness and ability" to do everything in life. To assure this would mean the *a priori* failure of the educational forming of our pupils. But "willing and able" does have another meaning.

Every individual sustains various relationships in life. In each of these relationships he has his own place. We do not require every individual to be willing and able to fulfill all the functions proper to every area of life in which he finds himself. In the church not every member is fit to be an elder; in the state not every citizen is suited to become a cabinet member; and in the realm of social affairs, not every worker can be the leader of a labor union. God does not demand maximum fitness and readiness for the performance of each and every important task within the several areas of life. It may be true that there are some persons to whom, it would seem, a special supernatural gift (charism), has been granted enabling them to fulfill a leading function in every sphere of life. And it may even be that in some of these instances character often plays a great, but not always praiseworthy role. It is certain, however, that we never demand of everyone to be "able and willing" to fulfill every function in every area of life's relationships. This is equally true on the higher and lower levels of life. Not every individual has to be qualified to be an elder in the church, but neither does everyone have to qualify as a deacon, an usher, or a janitor. Every person does not have to possess the qualities of a cabinet member, nor may we expect every individual to have the necessary fitness for distributing political propaganda leaflets.

After all, in our definition we spoke of "ability and willingness" to use one's own talents!

Rather it is a question of "fitness and readiness" to occupy cheerfully one's position in a given area of life's relationships. In determining this peculiarly individual place in life, it is of greatest significance that each individual examine his conscience before God with respect to the demands made upon him.

If someone is a church member, then he should be ready to fulfill the function for which he is qualified. But if God has also given this individual talents in many other areas, then his readiness, in the final analysis, is a matter of his own conscience. If a person who is playing an important role in political and social affairs is chosen to become an elder in the church, then he must determine before his own conscience whether or not he can accept this office. If he decides that he does not have a moment's free time at his disposal, then it is a question for his own conscience to determine whether he will ask to be released from the office of elder, or whether he must decline some political or social function. "Fitness" and "readiness," therefore, do not imply that the individual must do everything which he may be qualified to do, or even everything he may be assigned to do. For that would mean that a person would gradually lose his personality and finally no longer be a personality. Thus if a professor were to receive eighty letters each day, his "fitness" and "readiness" to answer those letters certainly does not imply that he should answer all those letters. Whether or not he answers them will depend upon how he conscientiously believes he should allot his time. The division of his time and effort cannot be determined by random correspondents who do not have the least responsibility for his time scheduling.

From the foregoing we conclude that the goal of education must be: to so form the individual that he is able and willing to assume responsibility for his God-given talents and qualifications by active participation in various areas of life. Thus "willingness" has reference to *the inclination for self-surrender.* "Fitness" relates to the practical forming of the individual in those areas in which he possesses native capacities. But "readiness" and "fitness" may not be detached from the fact that the person in question is a personality who serves God in accordance with what *he* knows to be *his* duty in his particular place in life.

Thus far we have spoken in the main about the goal of education as it concerns the pupil. However, we should not overlook the fact that in the background of all education there is a further purpose: namely, the maintenance of the structure of life's relationships in which we are placed by God. In the education of the individual we shall have to keep in mind the respective provinces of the church, state, society, culture, art, and science. Therefore, education must always be related to these distinct spheres of life.

Because of its relationship to the aforementioned spheres of life, pedagogy is under necessity of developing and specializing in a two-fold direction.

On the one hand, we shall have to examine how the educational objective can serve the state, society, culture, art, and science. On the other hand, we must face the question how the aim of education may be related to any one of these spheres in the educational forming of any particular individual. This is not to be construed in the sense that there is a special type of education which prepares a man for the state, another kind of education which fits him for culture, and still another which forms him for art. But it does mean that the talent in a particular child may require special emphasis on a particular form and aspect of education. Education at a theological seminary is specifically training for the church; education at a school of music is in particular training for art; education at a university is training for science. It is possible to say that instruction at any particular kind of school is to a certain extent also training with a view to culture and likewise with a view to the state and society. We are dealing here with aspects of educational training which lend individual nuances to the aim of education.

In nearly every instance, an element of general education is derived from all of these areas. A good Christian training in the home is not detached from the catechetical and religious training which the church gives with a view to the church. The aim of that training is also to make of the child a good citizen, to assist him in securing a good posititION in society, and to put him in possession of a certain cultural heritage. These aims are sought to enable the child to maintain himself in life, to enable him to enjoy the art of others, to enable him to understand the first principles of science, or to have access to the benefits of science.

But everyone will understand that the facts formulated here are already included in the definition which we gave for the aim of education. All of this is implicit in the statement "able and willing" to use one's talents to the honor of God and to the welfare of mankind in every area of life in which we are placed by God. Thus all these areas of life are already as a matter of principle in our definition of the objective of education.

With regard to special training such as that given at a theological seminary, at an art or music institute, or at a university, it must be said that these do not properly belong in a definition of the aim of Christian education in general. For precisely at this point we move from a general to a very particular area.

There is, however, another fact to consider. It is possible to reverse the proposition, as I began to do initially, and to say that every particular area of life has a primary interest in the maintenance of the right educational objective. Without the right kind of education, no single area of life can maintain itself. In a nation without education, culture and learning die, society becomes disrupted, and the state perishes. And in such an instance, the church threatens to become a community of rather sombre-looking conservatives.

But now we are also able to defend the proposition that there is no area of life which is not influenced by the nature of education. The sound formulation of the aim of education and its practical application according to this sound definition in all of our training will result in growth in church and state, in society and culture, in art and science.

Needless to say, in this manner any particular area of life and any particular manifestation of life will immediately be pervaded by the spirit in which the children are educated. If anyone wishes to build a Christian culture, he can do this only with persons who have received a Christian education. Whoever desires a society in which the basic idea of Christianity is not daily made a scandal, must understand well that he can only begin to approach his ideal when the education which children receive conforms to the framework of his ideal definition. It is foolish to think that we can get a society conforming to the claims of Christianity when our children receive a liberal, communistic, or pragmatic education. All propaganda in such a society is thwarted due to the fact that the citizens have no inner contact with the ideals which we pursue. From youth on, these citizens have no spiritual affinity with the spirit which we desire to find in their lives.

Thus the aim of education encompasses all of life, every manifestation of life. It also encompasses the future of the church, the future of the state, and the future of society. Educational objectives have a penetrating power which extends to, and is reflected in, our museums, schools, and theatres. The general aim of education is written large on advertising billboards, in dramatic plays, and in television shows.

Therefore, the formulation of the goal of education is of such great significance for the entire life of the nation. Without question it is true that the basic principles underlying various definitions differ. But he who takes his position upon the Word of God knows, on the one hand, that his statement of objectives is the most inclusive conceivable: it encompasses life and death; it encompasses this age and the world to come; it encompasses heaven and earth; it encompasses God and the creature; it exceeds the limits of time and space.

This implies that by the adoption of our statement of objectives, we engage in a struggle; we come to grips with the conflict of opinions also within the pale of the nation. But we cannot do less, for Jesus Christ has come into the world to establish a crisis.

And on the other hand, if the object of education is right, that objective also inevitably serves the interest and welfare of the community at large. For however much we resist the idea which makes demonstrable, concrete utilitarianism a norm in formulating the goal of education, nevertheless, we uphold the idea that the element of utilitarianism may not be overlooked in a definition of the essence of Christian education. Godliness is profitable unto all things. There can be no society which is more purposive than one in which men live according to the ordinances of God.

This point of view does not mean that in essence we disrupt the unity of the nation. As a matter of principle that rupture is present. Indeed, there is a demarcation between those who live according to the revelation of God and those who make man the norm and measure of all things. But it is peculiarly characteristic of the Christian view of life that its objective encompasses the unity of the nation. For they who live according to the Word of God as sheep amidst the wolves have every intention of being the salt of the earth and the light upon the candlestick. They are the salt of the earth, and they know that the salt works only if it penetrates the food. They desire to expend all their energy also for the national objective, so that within the national community and a unified society a basis may be found for the development and growth of Christian life. It is their desire that this world shall be so constituted that it may form the background for the growth of the congregation of the Lord until the day in which Jesus Christ shall return upon the clouds. In this way the congregation of believers serves not only the church, but also the state; not only society, but also culture; not only art, but also science. And in serving God thus, they witness that *from him, through him, and unto him are all things.* To God be glory through all eternity.

3

Authority, Discipline, and Freedom in Christian Education

IN SPEAKING of authority, discipline, and freedom in Christian education, we again come to grips with one of those typically pivotal questions about which the whole problem of modern education turns. Our discussion of this question will have to be as thetical as possible; for if, within the given time limitations, we wished merely to list all the opinions we must reject, we should not be able to set forth our own views. Consequently, I shall actually refer only occasionally to those whose opinions I do not share, even though their opinions are the background of what I say.

When we speak of educators, it stands to reason that in the first place we think of parents; in many instances we even think of them exclusively. Accordingly, the things I have to say will, as a matter of principle, apply in the fullest sense to both the parental authority and discipline, and to the freedom accorded the child by its parents.

In our approach to the problems of authority, we must begin by affirming that the authority to educate is always a derived authority. I have no right to exercise authority over a child which I encounter at random. The right "to be an educator" always presupposes a relationship of law to the one to be educated. This relationship to the young person to be educated is not in the first place the outcome of a voluntary decision on the part of the educator. (Sometimes it may be necessary to require such a voluntary decision, however.) But the person who educates another always does so by virtue of a mandate. "Being an educator" is always characterized by the fulfillment of a moral mandate; almost always its character is that of fulfilling an official mandate.

When a child comes into the home, a specifically parent-child relationship develops. That relationship is not described by stating that the parents are obligated to educate and guide the child, for whose life they are responsible, merely out of social considerations. We may grant the presence of such considerations, but they do not reach the heart of the matter. We might state it as follows: Parents who do not think they have a calling to nurture and guide the child which they have engendered and brought into the world (extreme radical view), have no conception of their task and calling; but neither do those parents have this who regard their task to consist merely in sustaining the child's life and in aiding the child to make the most of itself, and that simply because the child owes its existence to them (bio-sociological view). It is all wrong to say that education (*opvoeding*: nurture) implies only: bearing the consequences of the fact that you have brought a child into the world; and that education is merely the natural consequence of being the biological cause for the coming into existence of another human being. If education was truly only the result of that fact, then those who educate could content themselves with sustaining the life of the child and forming and directing him in such a manner that presently the child could maintain his own existence; in that case education would signify merely activity within the biological sphere. Fortunately, most parents feel that they have greater obligations. The special tie between parents and children is much more than is comprised in the statement: parents are the natural cause for the existence of the child and therefore they have obligations.

We know the parent-child relationship in life is included in a special ordinance of God for life. That special ordinance of God is linked up with the Covenant in which God includes both parents and children. And it is fortunate that thousands and thousands of parents still feel there is something unique about the parent-child relationship even though they may possess no knowledge of the Covenant of God. Many persons try to explain that uniqueness exclusively in terms of natural relationships. They say it is natural for parents to be fond of their children and consequently to desire to do everything possible for both the physical and spiritual well-being of their children. Those who speak thus think that the activities of parents, the educational or nurturing activity (in a physical and spiritual sense) is based on natural parent-child relationships.

I may observe, however, that this view of the matter merely transfers the problems to another area. Indeed, what is the cause of the love of the parents for their children? Why is there such a very special tie between parents and children? How does one explain the fact that these parents from the very outset feel responsibility toward their children; that their love impels them to such a degree that they can do nothing but seek that which is best for the physical and spiritual welfare of their children?

Everyone will realize that the simple fact of physical unity between parents and children is not enough to explain the parents' wish to educate. It has been said that the explanation must be sought in the fact that man is a rational being, and that this rationality naturally leads him to educate, that is, to bring up the child. I should like to make two observations against this view. In the first place, the spiritual education of the child on rational grounds as a rule results in bad education. When the educating takes place intuitively, it usually is better, even though it remains true that intuitive education of the spirit must be enriched by insight. But that is quite another matter. The point is we find it to be a fact that parental training which is based purely on rational grounds is worse than that based on intuitive grounds, that is, the inner compulsion which motivates the parents in educating their children. And in the second place, it is a remarkable phenomenon, that when pure rationality governs life, the tie between parents and children becomes weakened and the parental urge to educate the child decreases. Cold rationality which leads men to act, because the actions can be reasoned out, as a matter of fact, makes the urge to act less and less in every area of life. Phenomena, observable in our own society, make it plain moreover, that rational insight can never be the basis—at least not a good basis—for educational activity.

In the relationship between the educator and the one to be educated—in so far as it relates to the relationship: parents-children—there is always a two-fold aspect: first, the educator's love for the child; second, the educator's awareness of responsibility toward the child of today who must become the man of tomorrow.

It goes without saying, that these two elements of love and a feeling of responsibility must be present in educators in general, and consequently also in them to whose care children have been entrusted.

This very typical element of the feeling of responsibility now leads us to the heart of the matter in our discussion of the task of the educator. Why is the educator conscious of his responsibility? Why does he know that he is responsible for what happens to the child? Surely, it is because he is aware of having a mandate. This feeling of responsibility cannot be attributed to a general feeling of responsibility present in the social community. That I should assume responsibility for a child which stands on the river-bank and threatens to fall into the river, while I am in a position to prevent that accident, is abundantly clear. In this case, however, my responsibility is of a general character. Whether it is a helpless child I can save or a drunken man makes no difference at all. What is involved is my relationship to a fellow human being. But when a person is the educator of a child or of a youth, then the relationship is a very special one. That special relationship may have a two-fold character.

There may be a very specific relationship between this educator and that pupil, as in the case of a foster-father and a foster-son; or again between a teacher and one particular boy in his section who requires special attention. Furthermore, the relationship may be one of the educator's responsibility toward a group. But as soon as we begin to speak of the role of the educator, we shall always find a specific responsibility towards a particular individual under particular circumstances. This responsibility also has a permanent character. Otherwise there can be no question of educating. An official "who must look after a boy," is not an educator: he is a guard.

Accordingly, we observe that the element of responsibility always comes to the fore in education. But now it remains true that this responsibility can be realized only by way of love. If the educator does not feel attached to the child or young person he must educate, the task of educating will fail. Without this love it is not possible to understand the child. Moreover, the educator will lack the necessary patience if he does not have love. But the most important thing is this: without love there is missing in the education that unique quality which causes the child to respond to the educational process. Education without love is nothing more than the issuing of commands. But commands do not educate, they only drill; they can make of the human being a clever creature, which knows all the loopholes of the law, but they do not form personality. Therefore education without love—assuming for a moment that this were possible—is such a tremendous danger to the child and even to society. Education without love produces automatons or permanent rebels against the social order, or formally correct but inhibited persons who dare not express themselves, or other such types.

There are, therefore, two elements without which the educator cannot teach: love and a feeling of responsibility.

Now it is possible to relate the feeling of one's responsibility directly to a mandate. I am responsible for something, but also to someone. And indeed no responsibility is conceivable without this relationship to the person to whom I am responsible for something or for someone. The feeling of responsibility is determined by this personal relationship.

I intentionally did not speak of the authority of parents until now. Indeed, if we state that love and a feeling of responsibility are the distinctive characteristics out of which educational activity grows, then we regard the activity of the parents differently than if we say they are invested with authority. Moreover, it is not possible to equate love and authority, as though they were of coordinate importance. It is frequently done, but that does not make it right. Frequently one hears it said that authority and love are both necessary in education. Now in itself this is true, but you are making a mistake when you coordinate love and authority as two entities more or less independent from each other.

We now wish to address ourselves to the question: How are these two characteristics of the educator, his authority and his love, mutually related?

There is no easy answer to this question, the more so because it is evident that in the practice of everyday living there are such persistent misconceptions of this matter. For many people the parent-child relationship is such that parents should state: "It is natural for me to love you, and besides God has invested me with authority"; or else: "I love you and you are called upon to obey me"; or again: "I have been given authority, and you must love me, your educator, so that you may receive my love in return." This problem of authority in education we intend to examine more closely, noting particularly both the relationship of authority and love, and the relationship of that authority to the feeling of responsibility in the educator.

No one will dispute the following proposition: God has given parents authority over children, and therefore—stated otherwise—God has given particular parents authority over the young persons who are to be educated. If I state the proposition that parents (that is, educators) love their children and should love them, no one will object. Nor will anyone deny the proposition that God has entrusted the children (who are his children) to the parents for their education, and that therefore they are responsible for those children. Nevertheless, we are making a mistake when we continue to speak of these as three distinct matters: the authority of the educator, the love of the educator, and the feeling of responsibility of the educator. These differentiations which can so easily become differences have had many unfortunate results.

What is the essential character of being an educator? It is: "to fulfill a mandate." God has given the parents a mandate to bring up their children. That is a duty of the parents. From this follows their responsibility. To enable the parents to fulfill their obligation, God has vested in the parents that which they need for fulfilling their duty. And what is that? Is it possible in answer to say: on the one hand they are in need of authority and on the other hand they are in need of love? I hold that it is not so, and when I say this I know someone will wish to contradict me. But I also know that on the basis of God's Word I am convinced that I may not hold anything else. Authority and love are not a duality in education. Parental authority cannot be separated from parental love. In many respects they are even indistinguishable, because authority is love and love is authority. I would also be prepared to defend the proposition that good authority never can be divorced from love. He possesses authority who has the final say, who can lay down the law. But among human beings only he has the final say who is bound to his fellows by inner ties. Without this inner tie, authority becomes tyranny! Consequently, no sooner does parental authority become dissociated from parental love in the consciousness of the child, or separated from the love which the child feels toward the parents, before the authority begins to miscarry. And the parents will have to understand and put this in practice every day.

Conversely, love can never be detached from authority. Love which is not at all times and in all places an expression of the task of the parents, who bear that authority, is not genuine love. Such love of the educator soon becomes coddling, soon becomes a soft-hearted indulging of the whims and wishes of the child. Such authority loses its connection with the law of God.

Here we touch upon another point which shows how harmoniously interwoven authority and love are. We now refer in particular to authority and love as they become evident in education. The concept of "law" is correlative with that of "authority." Authority demands obedience. Authority is related to the rule which we must obey, the law which calls for obedience. In the awareness of many individuals it is particularly this fact which causes an inner separation of love and authority. They say: the law commands, the law is severe, the law is cold. Love binds, love is compassionate, love is warm, and therefore the love-side of authority is evangelical. The law side of authority is legal, Old-Testament-like, and essentially it is a thing that has been transcended.

He who speaks so has no understanding of the essence of law. In our discussion of moral education, I hope to refer to this point again. However, I wish to make the observation here and now that the law of God is an expression of God's being, and hence also an expression of the love of God by which he is bound to His own cosmos. If the creature lives according to the law, the ordinance, the rule which God has laid down for His creatures, then all will be well with that creature. The creature of God will experience that the law of God is nothing but the expression of a rule which enables the creature to find and maintain its life. The law of love is like the loving human hand which casts the fish which has floundered upon dry land back into the water; it is the love whereby one human being saves another from drowning. The law is not present to chastise us, to make us unhappy, to rob us of freedom, but the law is there to show us the way along which we can go to life, to the light. The law points us to the place where it is safe and where we can be happy.

To be sure, if we acknowledge the law in this sense, then we also presuppose that other function of the law by which we know our misery and whereby the law itself becomes our schoolmaster to Christ. But in Christ that law becomes to us a rule of life; the law becomes for us an expression of the love of God. Therefore the legal side of the authority is exactly the same as the love side.

But it is evident that on this view I cannot regard authority in education as something different from love. Indeed, the correct exercise of authority by the educator is only possible, is in fact only permissible, when carried out in love; but to this authority in love and to this love in authority there remains conjoined a responsibility. This is also true because of the fact that in bringing up our children, we are dealing with something which is not our possession, but God's possession. God says to all children of the Covenant: "You are my children," even when parents degenerate so far that they offer their children to Moloch.

Now, however, the question arises as to whether this authority of the parents, interdependent as it is with their love, and their love as well, are dependent upon the subjective recognition by the child. A parallel question is: to what extent does the law of God demand our obedience, even if we are not able to render that obedience out of love?

In answering the question as to the validity of authority, we must begin by declaring that the exercise of authority may never be such that there is a separation between love and authority. If this unity is broken in the one who bears authority, then he is on the way to misusing that authority; and if he continues on that path, he will finally arrive at the point where he must be deprived of the authority. The fact that authority and love are one in education by no means signifies that the child or young person subject to parental authority now also has the right to reject the authority. He should obey his parents out of love. But he may not say: "If such love is lacking, I am no longer obliged to obedience, for in that case my obeying would only be a slavish obedience." If a young person were to argue in this manner, he certainly would demonstrate his lack of understanding of this relationship. The authority of love, which is exercised over him with loving authority, is balm for his loving heart; and if he obeys out of love, then all is well. But if he does not wish to obey, because he has no love, then authority remains, nonetheless. Authority exercised in the spirit of love—that most certainly is the essence of parental authority; however, this does not imply that the child who supposes he cannot respond in love by the same token does not have to acknowledge the authority of his parents. Every child must see the authority of his parents as representative of the authority of God. God's authority too is an authority in love. Therefore, rejection of that love is equivalent to defiance of God himself and consequently of his authority. Likewise, he who disclaims the love of his parents, attacks their authority, and hence the parents themselves. This also signifies that they who do not acknowledge the authority of love stand guilty before their parents, and that therefore by virtue of the parental authority and love they must receive punishment.

Accordingly, parents who understand their authority and the significance of that authority, will be expected to take disciplinary measures in due course when a child by disobeying shows its lack of love. Consequently the authority of the parents continues even when their love is rejected by the child.

And a child, therefore, who no longer recognizes the authority of its parents as an authority of love, can expect nothing less than to experience the parental authority either as a compelling authority or as a punitive authority. In such a case what has really happened is that the child who no longer has an eye for love and accordingly rejects authority in its further contacts with that authority no longer experiences the love which is present. And the child suffers punishment in the name of this authority (which nevertheless really remains an expression of love) in order that the child may come to acknowledge that authority as the authority of love.

Although we must regard the authority of the parents as the authority of love, yet we must not overlook the fact that this authority as such also results from a God-given mandate. We should not, however, regard this mandate as one which God, after giving many other mandates and talents, now adds as a special mandate, namely, that of authority over children. Indeed not. But it does mean that in the entire covenantal relationship, authority, love, and responsibility appear as a unity. As God is one in all his virtues, so in the relation of God to his children the demand comes that we in turn experience the unity of all those virtues which God in the covenantal relationship is pleased to grant his children for their covenantal task.

As far as our analytic reasoning is concerned, it may very well be true that there is a duality in authority and love, and that it is extremely difficult to think of these two as a unity. But as opposed to this, it is equally true that in a believing acceptance of the covenantal mandate these two are indeed one; and further that in their oneness with the feeling of responsibility they form a unity for the practice of life.

Authority and love, therefore, constitute a unity. The discipline which the parents exercise over the child stems from this unity. This exercise of discipline is first of all a question of the day to day attitude of the parents. The child of the Covenant, who is to be educated in the way of the Covenant, must continually be seen as a covenantal child. That is not to say that we should have to speak of the Covenant to the child each day. Indeed, this should not be done until the child has reached at least the years of discretion. But the attention of the child should be called on the one hand to the love of God, to the love of Christ, who loved and still loves him; and on the other to the fact that he must now also love God, that he must realize his need for forgiveness from sin, and that he should ask God to love him in spite of the fact that his heart is sinful. In all Christian education this apparent duality is in truth a unity. And it is precisely the same duality and the same unity which the educator finds in his own life. It is the duality and unity found in the declaration: "all my sins have been forgiven" and in the petition: "forgive us our debts."

Now education must primarily be of such a character that the child experiences in its educators, hence particularly in the parents, the truth described above. The entire life's attitude of mother and father, of teacher and master should manifest itself to the child as a daily walking with God. That is something quite different from the attitude revealed by some Christians who represent God only as an avenging justice, whom the child must fear, and whom you must placate from hour to hour by taking care that you do not sin against his commands.

On the one hand, discipline has bearing on the fact that the parents, in particular the educator, and even more particularly the father and mother, must give guidance to the child in growing up. Discipline has reference to restraining or bridling, but not exclusively in a negative sense; discipline is also a bridle which steers in the right path. On the other hand, it is just because the right path must be travelled and because the direction of that path is determined by both the starting-point and the end-point, that discipline is also a means to attain that end. One aspect of discipline is always the desire to attain the ideal. That is the specific character of pedagogical discipline. But as a pedagogical discipline it also includes a third aspect:

its purpose to bring the child to the point where he no longer requires discipline by others, and where self-discipline will enable the child to be his own guide. That is, of course, self-guidance according to the norms laid down in the Word of God.

In discipline, therefore, there is a confrontation of educator, child, and educational objective. Discipline is a means of education. Really it can be said that discipline is the only means of education, if the word discipline is rightly understood. "Discipline" is something wholly different from what is usually designated as a "disciplinary measure." Every means by which a child is guided in the right direction is a means of discipline. If in teaching, we teach a child the most simple rules of arithmetic, this is a means of disciplining the native capacity of the child in arithmetic to the laws which hold for arithmetic. Likewise, it can even be said that a child who learns a series of irregular French verbs is being disciplined; for only in this way will the child be able to curb himself from exceeding the bounds of grammar when speaking French. Obviously, the word discipline is used here in its broadest sense. But we are deliberate in stating that this is all discipline. Indeed, in this manner we include under discipline the proper regard for correct social manners, correct speech, and correct behavior in society. Unruliness, that is, the want of discipline, usually begins at the periphery of human existence. This initial lack of discipline often is related to the lack of respect for the little things which make our societal life pleasant. People who always appear too late at meetings, who always speak a little longer than their alloted time, or people who go to bed boisterous and late while staying at a hotel, or who whisper during a concert, these people have not disciplined their lives. And as a matter of course, the attitude of such individuals finds its reflection in their children. In children, and particularly in the youth of our time, there is, generally speaking, a serious lack of discipline.

A want of discipline is not restricted to vandalism: the destruction of shrubbery in park or garden, or the smashing of windows; but a lack of discipline is also demonstrated when someone plays a noisy jazz record for hours in a rooming house full of guests, or when a group of campers troops into church just three minutes late. If parents and educators do not have an open eye for these matters, and accordingly allow children the so-called freedom to have their fling, with the resulting disturbance to other people in the community, then this points to a faulty conception of discipline and one which will have very serious consequences. Expressions such as: "Its nobody else's business," or "People shouldn't be offended so quickly," or "If I think it is fun, why shouldn't I do it?" reveal an attitude of mind which is basically undisciplined.

We do not intend, of course, to suggest that the child must be educated in a strait-jacket. Far from it. All education, also education in discipline, requires freedom. Discipline serves to protect freedom.

What is freedom? Freedom is not: "severance of all bonds." A fish is free only when it swims in water; it is bound to the water. A bird enjoys freedom only when it can fly in the air; it is bound to space. Accordingly, there are certain bonds which belong to the nature of every living being. As soon as we overlook this in discussing the concept of "freedom" we go astray in defining the character of true freedom.

A living creature lacks freedom only when it is bound by bonds which do not belong to its nature. A bird without air, or a fish without water, lacks freedom even though in all other respects it is free. They are free only by virtue of the bonds which belong to their nature. There are many bonds which do not belong to our essential humanity. If a man is bound by such bonds, he lacks freedom. But there are other bonds which are an essential part of our humanity. In the absence of these bonds, man lacks freedom as much as the fish which is outside the bonds of water. Thus the human individual is bound by such clothing as befits the climate in which he lives. Man is likewise bound by certain social bonds. The child who prematurely frees himself from the parental bond does not gain freedom, but rather loses freedom; this is true because the bond between this child and its parents is a natural relationship which the child needs if it is to develop and give full scope to its natural gifts. Most human beings fortunately are bound to a person of the opposite sex by the very special bond of love. This being bound belongs to the nature of man and only in this restrictive bond can man truly be free; only in this being bound can he live his life to the full. There are a few individuals who are not capable of love. For them the marriage-bond means the loss of freedom. Likewise, the marriage-bond between two persons of opposite sexes which is not based on an essential compatibility of the marriage partners results in a loss of freedom.

Thus we conclude that freedom means: the rejection of those bonds which are foreign to essential nature; but that freedom also implies: the acceptance of those bonds which belong to essential nature.

Accordingly, we are now able to state that child-discipline has as its purpose the averting of all those bonds which are foreign to the essential nature of the child in general, and to this child in particular; but discipline must also serve to strengthen and fortify all the bonds which are inherent in the child in general, and inherent in any particular child. And this must take place in such a way that the child learns to be happy without those bonds which are foreign to his nature and happy with those bonds which are peculiar to his nature.

Now societal living is one of those bonds which is characteristic of the nature of the child. And the child can feel happy only if his organic adjustment to society has been made in a harmonious way. Therefore discipline of the child also signifies that in all of his societal relationships, the child learns to live in a manner conformable to the nature of any given group or community, and so to reveal his membership in that community.

Naturally, this discipline cannot be achieved unless the child has experienced the "spirit" of a particular group. That is to say, that he learns to adapt himself to such an extent, that his feeling, the totality of his being is sensitized, as it were, to discover the *tendenz* which prevails in any particular locale. That is necessary if the child is to learn to shun any particular kind of fellowship which is wrong for him, or which in itself has a wrong purpose. Such a discipline must be practised with patience in quiet conversation with the child. But this exercise in discipline also implies that the child himself must learn to take a position with respect to the group or community. Although we do not wish to suggest that it is possible in the case of every child, yet it is the ideal of good discipline that the child learn not only to feel his way into the group or community, but that he also learns to maintain his personal independence and his critical judgment with respect to that group or community.

Moreover discipline simultaneously has as its goal that the child may learn to restrain his inclinations, desires, passions, and instincts. It stands to reason that in relation to this objective habit-forming and habituation play an important part in the practice of living.

However, the principal goal of discipline is that the child may learn to subject himself obediently to the ordinances of God, and to do this in such a way that he daily experiences the law as love, also as love of God towards the individual child. Therefore disciplinary measures are justified only when the child experiences in that discipline the love of the disciplinarian. Every punishment given in a hot temper, every chastisement administered in a fit of anger, every scolding resulting from irritation on the part of father or mother, and every snubbing out of self-preservation or nervousness, has the wrong effect, and is, in fact, not Christian discipline.

From what has been said so far it could be concluded that although the disciplining of children should conform to general rules, it is not necessary to make further distinctions. Nothing could be farther from the truth. Anyone who educates is dealing with a child who has particular characteristics, individual qualities, individual ways of reacting and individual talents. In the general practice of education and in the exercise of discipline in particular, the educator very definitely must take into account who and what the child is. The first requirement of good discipline is that the child, as he is, does not get a feeling of discouragement through the discipline because he does not experience love in discipline.

But the immediate implication of this fact is also that there must be a very great differentiation and variation in the exercise of discipline. In calling attention to the following examples, we emphasize that they are to be regarded merely as illustrations. A boy of six years, robust and strong, and possessing a genuine sense of humor, who at a given moment consciously violates a command of his father, must undergo a form of discipline which is quite different from that given another six-year old boy, equally healthy, but who lacks a sense of humor and is more rigid and schematized in his actions. Perhaps this rigid schematism in the boy is even to be attributed to his parents. But in any case there is behind this schematism in the little child a kind of fear for life, for what life may bring. Schematic people are after all always persons who take refuge in schematization because they have a fear of not being equal to life; they take flight into schematization out of ignorance, anxiety, or fear. Now schematization always has a negative cause. It is possible for a six-year old to reveal already a tendency to do everything in such a rigidly schematized manner that you can notice his embarrassment when he is forced out of it. Such a child obviously is completely different from the boy who immediately reacts to a humorous situation and enjoys it. Let us say the boy with a sense of humor has an inclination to grab a cookie; he follows his inclination, takes the cookie and quickly eats it, but he is caught in the act. Then one might very well remark: that boy has taken a cookie and consequently a punishment must follow which suits a boy who steals a cookie. The same thing could be said for the second boy, the schematic one, the boy who is much more rigid. But it would be foolishness to think that punishment is something which can be administered according to the book: "The punishment fits the crime." It must also fit the criminal. Even a physician varies his prescriptions to fit the individual make-up of the patient. And when parents resort to punishment, they should take into consideration the type of child they are dealing with.

However, it is characteristic of such situations that the parents of the boy who has remained the humorous type are as a rule themselves responsible for the fact that their boy has a sense of humor; whereas in the case of the other child the parents themselves share responsibility for the fact that their six-year old boy takes flight into schematization. Needless to say, these situations make the problem difficult in practice, for in all likelihood the latter parents will also be inclined to proceed too schematically in exercising discipline because of the cookie; whereas the former parents may have an inclination to be lax in their discipline because they cannot help laughing at the "funny face" their boy pulls in his wrong-doing. It is necessary for the parents of both children to realize the background of the trespass of their child. Let us assume (by no means unlikely) that in the case of the humorous type of child the background is as follows: An attempt to see how far the boy can go in playing a trick on his parents. The only correct discipline in that event is for the parents to disrupt at once and without much ado the general feeling of good humor existing between them and the child; and that they then say: "No, that is not nice, that is not funny at all; now you really are making a nuisance of yourself; that is naughty, and if it happens again, we shall have to punish you." This child must learn to feel what is the difference between a joke and something which is really wrong. But in the case of the second boy, the situation very probably is different. We will assume that the following condition is present: This schematic child who has in his background certain fears of life and certain inhibitions toward father and mother, has the tendency to create his own little world in which he experiences a degree of pleasure in a manner agreeable to himself. Perhaps feelings of vengeance also play something of a role. Now if this child is severely punished—and schematic parents are apt to punish severely—then the child's feeling of being isolated will be aggravated, and his feeling of vengeance will be intensified. And further, if the child is given a long lecture on the sin of stealing, he will again feel the punishment to be within the same schematization in which he has been trained all the while. Therefore, when mother notices that her child has helped himself to a cookie, it is quite possible that she would do best to put her arm around her son and say: "My boy, did you really want a cookie that badly? You may ask mother for one, but don't just help yourself; mother doesn't like that, and you shouldn't do it either. You know that, don't you? Tonight mother will give you another cookie." We have called attention to these two examples to demonstrate how the same offense may require different forms of discipline, even in the case of comparatively young children. The purpose of discipline is always to preserve, to teach the child to go in the right path. Therefore, the exercise of discipline surely does not always imply chastising, punishing. To exercise discipline signifies: to take that measure which is needed to bring the child to self-discipline. Consequently, the idea of some Christian parents who think they sin if they do not punish a certain violation of their child is wholly erroneous.

Sometimes to forgive is a much better means of discipline than to spank. That likewise depends upon the nature of the child and the nature of the wrong. In this connection it should be emphatically emphasized that in all disciplining and particularly in all punishing one must consider what the child has really done. We should not forget that we exercise discipline upon the child and not upon the deed of the child.

By discipline we must always attempt to reach the inner self of the child. Discipline must not be measured in terms of the more or less accidental external situation. Therefore discipline must always be exercised with much understanding of the inner attitude of the child toward his parents and toward the command, and thus toward him who gives the command. It is a serious mistake on the part of many parents that they do not have an eye for these matters. Perhaps it is necessary for us to admit that unfortunately the sin of many educators is their use of discipline solely as a ruler or measuring line which, moreover, is applied only to external situations. In this manner, however, discipline works inversely and accordingly the child develops a dislike for the commandment. For then he gets the feeling that the law is not love, but hate; that the law is not life, but the severance of life, that it is death to all that lives.

If discipline must be exercised in different ways for different children, then it also follows that in the form and content of disciplinary measures we should take into consideration the age of the children. The educator should possess, as it were, the gift of growing up with the child in the educational activities. The exercise of discipline here also comes into immediate contact with moral education, although not exclusively with it; in every branch of pedagogical activity it is always necessary to demand maximum achievement of the child when it is a question of the child subordinating his life to a form of self-discipline. When it is possible to persuade the child to do something good or to avoid something bad from considerations arising out of the content of his own life, the discipline will possess far greater value, viewed pedagogically, than when the child has been obedient in response to some advice, to some rebuke previously given by the parents. There are very many extremely obedient children who are obedient until they are twenty years old, but who are of no significance for the rest of their lives. Whether it is due to innate disposition, or whether it is due to their education, they have not been brought to the point of confronting life as independent individuals. The exercise of discipline will always have to be directed toward enabling the child to make his own decisions. Not until this choosing of a position is clearly sinful, or is clearly harmful to the child, will it be necessary to resort to discipline.

It will be readily understood that in exercising discipline we must constantly keep in mind that the child is also a religious being. Discipline makes it final, if you will its highest, appeal to the religious nature of the child. This does not mean that the appeal consists exclusively in holding up to the child the command of God. Discipline makes an appeal to the entire personality in the totality of its attributes, characteristics, and qualities; and these are present only because the child is a religious being.

The various attributes of the individual such as trust, submissiveness, faith, devotion, control of natural inclinations, knowledge of God's will, awareness of life's potentialities, and experiential acquaintance with life — all of these must be viewed as an organic unity, proceeding from the ego and basically directed toward the service of God, but all of these qualities must also be incorporated into the life of discipline. The root of all discipline is to teach the child to understand "that you are not your own." That is one side of the matter. But there also is immediately and even simultaneously another side; not until our life is disciplined in submission to God and his service will our life be happy and peaceful; not until then can we live ourselves to the full and do the things we really like; not until then will our life become one with the life of the people about us; in fact, one with the life of all creation. The purpose of discipline is therefore ever and anew to teach the child to experience the love of God which comes to us in the law and ordinances; so that we, living in discipline, may see the light and may be able to live happily and contentedly. Viewed thus the expression "to kiss the rod" is intelligible. This is not the cringing attitude of the individual who caresses the punishing hand of the master and thus tries to compel friendliness, but it is the grateful attitude of the person who feels again the love of the Father and who has been brought back into that framework of life in which he only can find happiness.

4

Personality and Character Formation in Christian Education

We cannot think of "character" without at the same time thinking of "personality." A character always belongs to a personality, and there can be no personality without a character. Misunderstanding has sometimes arisen due to the fact that the word character is also used in a more special sense in an expression such as, "He is a man of character." The word "character" here means "strong" or "excellent" character. However, the use of the word "character" in this sense is not acceptable from a scientific point of view, although in daily life the word "character" can mean "strong character" and sometimes also "good character."

The word "character" has reference to that which gives color to personality and thus we refer to someone as a colorful or colorless personality. Character lends to personality that uniqueness which enables the personality, while in the presence of others, to manifest itself distinctively, and with varying degrees of intensity in diverse relationships.

Thus we observe that the word "character" is inseparable from the word "personality." Accordingly, it does not seem possible to me to develop a theory of character without an accompanying theory of personality. Indeed, if character is the color of personality, then the theory of character must correspond to the theory of personality. And what you say about character as the color of personality will depend entirely upon your view of personality and personality structures.

Now the word "personality," like the word "character," is employed in a two-fold sense. The word "personality" is pregnant with meaning and it is also used in the sense of "a strong personality." Obviously, our discussion is not concerned with that concept. But we do wish to point out that this "special" concept of personality is much closer to a scientific concept than is the two-fold use of the word "character." If we say of a person, "he is a real personality," then this usually means that he is a "strong personality." But the word personality can also be used in the meaningful sense of designating a particular individual whose personality is well-ordered; or a well-balanced person, a person whose inner development has been harmonious. And in these instances the word "personality" indeed refers to matters of which we can and do speak in a scientific manner.

Originally "person" referred to the mask worn by actors. The actor's voice sounded through the mask. "Persona" is a derivation of the word used for mask. But it was not long before the word for mask began to have reference to the role which was being enacted. Thus one could ask, "Which mask are you playing?" that is, "which role are you playing?" As the word "persona" gradually lost its meaning as mask, it came to refer increasingly to the concept of "role." And so in time "persona" began to have reference to the individual being depicted. "Persona" therefore, referred to that other person who was being impersonated. But in the consciousness of the spectators the one who is being impersonated is that person himself. And once the word "persona" had come to mean "a role," but always signifying the man behind the mask, the individual being impersonated, it was very simple to arrive at the final change in meaning, that of the individual who is fulfilling his role. Thus "persona" signifies: the individual who fulfills a task, who has an independent position, who stands on his own in life.

Quite obviously, one is in error if he continues to associate the original meaning of "mask" with person. The word "personal," moreover, does not mean "masklike" or anything of the kind; but it means the individual who is able to be "someone" in his life, who can be a person, play "his own role," fulfill a task.

What then is a personality? A personality is a human being whose life can be said to be well integrated and well regulated.

By integration we mean that the various qualities of the individual—his talents, natural inclinations, aspirations, feelings, emotions, passions (mental content), and the like, are properly ordered and harmoniously related; that as a unity these qualities distinguish the individual from the environment, whereas collectively they are adapted to life. A good regulation of these relationships has been achieved when the ego of the individual controls his psychical assets—his natural inclinations, native talent, innate passions, and the like. Moreover, the hierarchy of those psychical properties in psychical life is determined by the balanced relations among the inner values of those properties, as they relate to the specific circumstances in which those relations are experienced.

The right kind of personality is master of its own psychical properties (although remaining subject to the power and authority of God, naturally, since man is a religious being), for the ego dominates in such a manner that there is an harmonious adjustment to the variable factor of time and place.

As we have previously seen, conscience is also a part of personality. One of God's gifts to the human personality is an immediate self-consciousness of its moral status as a living being.

If we examine the hierarchy of the personality structure of the human individual, we shall find uppermost the "ego," created by God, according to the Scriptures, and dominating in the microcosmos of individual human existence. The status of the relationship of this "ego" to God is decisive for the human individual. The regenerated ego directs itself to God on high. The unregenerate ego turns itself toward the cosmos and toward self. With his "ego" as subject, the human being experiences all that he is as being his own; but everything he experiences is experienced by him in a definite form, governed by definite norms, and bound by definite relationships. This typical form in which the personality expresses itself, in consequence of the peculiar structure of its psychical relationships (talents, inclinations, *etc.*), produces an individual wholly unique, a personality with a color all its own.

And this color we designate as character.

The problem of the forming of personality and character cannot be separated from the question of the forming of volitional life. However, it would take us too far afield if we were to discuss here all the problems which relate to the forming of volitional life. I merely wish to point out that we should not regard the will as an extension of reason or feeling, but rather as an individual area of psychical life. Although any human action can influence the volitional act, yet the volition remains an independent activity of the ego, and we should regard it as an active choosing by the subject. Therefore the human individual is also responsible for his volitions.

In the training of the will everything will hinge on the child's learning to choose both the right objective and the right means to attain that objective; and on his learning, from earliest youth, to be responsible for the selection of end and means, up to the measure of his insight and talents.

But we will not be able to treat this more extensively now. For if we did, we would also have to discuss how a person must learn to control his passions; and how the child at an early age already may be taught obedience to the commandment through the appropriate application of pedagogically formulated norms. But I shall come back to that problem later.

Matters are somewhat different in the question of moral training. Education in morality is of such great significance in the forming of personality and character that we shall have to make some comments on it.

There is, of course, a relationship between the forming of the will and moral training. But we shall have to restrict ourselves to merely calling attention to that relationship.

In commenting further on moral training, we wish to begin by observing that man is under all circumstances and at all times a moral being. The moral does not describe the positive character of an action, but the moral always describes, or qualifies, the individual who acts. Man is moral and therefore he can never do something which is not moral. Consequently his actions are always subject to the judgment: either good or evil.

In this connection we should bear in mind that the words "evil," "sin," "badness" do not refer to anything positive, to any actuality. On the contrary, these descriptions, "bad," "evil," "sin" point to the lack of positive qualities. It is a lack of that which one should possess.

However, even such an expression must be used accurately. Although in external appearance a person's action may be good, yet the person may be evil. And, on the contrary, an individual may be on a high moral level and still perform a deed which is bad. This points to the need of distinguishing between the person and his actions. Man himself always is and remains a moral being. The necessity of making a distinction between the moral status of the individual and the moral quality of his actions is very important for pedagogy. Presently we shall refer to this again.

The meaning of the moral qualification of the individual has frequently been misunderstood. The moral aspect of man was then limited to the area of direct obedience to the Ten

Commandments. The man who feared God and therefore did not swear, did not desecrate the Sabbath, and did not kill, thereby revealed his moral being; and if someone acted in just the opposite manner, he was sinning in the area of morals. However, this view often overlooked other moral delinquencies such as that of: the working-man who exerts himself just enough in his daily work to keep the boss from dressing him down; the merchant who mopes all day about the "hard lot of the small business-man"; the teacher whose unceasing complaint is about "the poor pay" in the teaching profession. Such a view does not take into consideration that one is morally delinquent if he is not conscious of an inner bond between work and calling. Morality, accordingly, is restricted to the direct pronouncements of the Decalogue. As a result of this viewpoint, moral education has often been seriously lacking in many respects. All too often it failed to regard as special objectives of moral training: (1) the moral bond between work and calling in life; (2) awareness of moral responsibility for all the actions of one's own personality. And consequently, in many of those circles which possessed "a positive Christian education" there was so little evidence of that genuine joy in living which is a product of Christian moral training. Indeed, moral training was not aimed at the practice of everyday life, but it was an attempt to keep the individual from evil in a variety of situations. Thus moral education was gradually reduced to a form of training which apparently could do little more than hold before the child with greatest possible force the prescript: "Touch not, taste not, handle not." And in this way, fear of sin, fear of evil, and fear of punishment came to be regarded as the most important moral incentives. But the psalmist's words: "How love I thy law, it is my meditation all the day" became less and less of a reality (Psalm 119: 97).

Now it is certain that moral training always has as its ultimate aim: obedience; and any thought of legalism should be banished from that obedience as well as any one-sided antinomianism. Knowing this is not enough, however. When one has learned that doing good is not meritorious as such and that he must reveal obedience to the law in doing good, he is not finished. Repeatedly he must ask the question: What is the essence of morality? And the Scriptures tell us that expressly: the essence of morality is love. Christ affirms with great emphasis that the law demands of us to love God above all and our neighbor as ourselves. Accordingly, the meaning of the law is not opposition to human existence, but the meaning of the law is precisely the preservation of that life through the Love of Him, who loves that life itself. And the moral aspect of man finds its culmination in his capacity to be bound to the ordinances of God in love.

But these ordinances of God should not be regarded merely as a few general rules for each and everyone. There is a special ordinance in the life of each individual. Man examines his own existence and within his own history he finds the order which God has fixed for his life. An artisan with limited ability has received both his ability and his vocation from God. That artisan would be acting against the moral order of his being if he did not care for his vocation and were jealous of someone more talented than he. This man too must experience that there is a moral tie between him and his work; and the true moral personality of this individual will not be disclosed until he succeeds in developing that attitude of mind in which he is genuinely amazed at the things he might accomplish in his vocation. Contentment with our God-given lot, willingness to fulfill our God-given place in life, these are essentially moral in nature.

Man must experience this moral tie in such a way that he is aware of his task as a part of himself. Obviously, we do not mean that his should be a pedantic attitude in the sense of: "Is not this the great Babylon that I have built?" But the situation should indeed be one in which he regards his own labor as a daily work of art wrought by him as God directed his actions and qualified his spirit, and wrought by him so that the Creator might be exalted in that work.

Thus from the very nature of the case, the concept of "ethical life" becomes much broader than when it refers exclusively to immediate obedience of the commands of the Decalogue. Without a doubt these matters are written in the Law, if only we read that Law rightly and understand it against its background, in the light of the entire Scriptures. For indeed, if we love God we also love his work in us, and in our heart a natural response to our daily task will develop; and it will develop, regardless of what our task is: whether it be digging of ditches, teaching children the difficulties of spelling, or preaching the Gospel of God in a fallen world.

It goes without saying that love of the command of God extends to all of life and all of life's relationships. We can speak of man's moral behavior in a positive sense only when it is in conformity with the Will of Him who is the Life, and in whose plan for life there is life indeed.

Now, for moral training it is of greatest importance to observe how the human individual becomes morally conscious, that is, therefore, how he comes in contact with the Law of God, with the work of God in his life. It is obvious that moral training is inseparable from the conscience. Several problems, by no means simple, arise at this juncture. And in discussing these problems it will be necessary for me to say a few things about character and character formation. We are confronted with the following question: how must we relate conscience to personality-structure? This question in turn relates to several other questions. Let us assume that an individual will have nothing to do with the Christian life-and-world view, that he is a full-fledged humanist; his actions moreover are quite consistent with his humanistic principles, for he does not regard them to be binding on his conscience only, but he acts in conformity with those principles. Of such an individual we must say: He has character. Nevertheless, it is quite possible that we are not all in agreement with his moral behavior. Perhaps his norms are different than ours. We are convinced that he is doing wrong, but at the same time we would not think of saying that he does not display real character. It is also conceivable that someone shares your views completely; indeed, he says he is bound in conscience as you are. However, you observe that this man does not act in conformity with his conscience. Even though he shares your outlook on life, you will say of such an individual: he lacks character. He has no real character and reveals no resoluteness of character. But even stronger: we can conceive of an individual who tells you that he disagrees with your norms, and that he possesses other norms. He says, further, that in his conscience he feels bound to *his* norms. But simply to do you a pleasure, on some matter of principle, he now does the thing you would like to have him do, while saying: "It is really against my conscience, but I want to do you a favor." Although this person may be doing exactly what you think he should do, you still would not regard him as resolute in character. Conceivably you might even tell him so and then he might reply: "Indeed, you are right, I have really acted against my conscience, and I am sorry." He now says that he is sorry about the deed of which you approve, and yet you, in judging his character, will consider this as being in his favor. How then are we to regard these relationships?

In our opinion, psychology must here distinguish carefully between personality and character. In dealing with personality, we are concerned first of all with the relationship between the various areas of talent and psychical content on the one hand, and the "ego" on the other hand. Whether or not an individual is a personality will be determined by the question of his integration and his regulation. Are the various psychical areas and psychical contents well ordered, and does the ego—as controlling factor—regulate this over-all personality in the appropriate manner? That question is decisive in the matter of the personality.

But within the totality of personality structure there is that which compels the personality to see itself as a moral person. The normal individual cannot help experiencing each day again that all his actions are subject to a judgment of good or bad. Man has an immediate, intuitive self-consciousness that life as such is moral. This awareness, as we have said, is intuited immediately. Man does not get it by way of experience, he does not secure it through education, but it is present to him, just as there is a self-consciousness of one's own rational existence; logical conclusions are called "natural," and a realistic view of the world is likewise designated as "natural." This rational self-consciousness is the basis for our submitting to reason. And the immediate, intuitive moral self-consciousness is the basis for man's daring to yield to his own actions.

This intuitive and immediate self-consciousness is the conscience. It belongs to the person. The human being has a conscience; but one could also state that the conscience has the individual. It exercises power, and rules, although not in the sense that the individual now experiences conscience as a separate entity. Indeed, it is a con-science, a knowledge beside the self, but viewed from another aspect it is exactly a self-knowledge about one's self. It is not correct to say that the voice of conscience is heard as an external voice protesting one's own action. On the contrary, each individual is in turn himself that other person. Anyone who does wrong hears the voice of conscience as another voice warning him. And the person who does the right thing hears the voice of conscience as another voice speaking its approval. In that case conscience seems something other. In listening to the voice of conscience, conscience becomes the "self": "I know that action was wrong," and then the acting individual becomes that other one. There is a constant interchange of subjects, as soon as the individual consciously applies the functioning of conscience to this or that activity. Accordingly, the conscience also belongs to the personality, and is an integral part of the personal being of the individual. Of course we can speak of a properly functioning conscience in the case of a given individual.

However, this does not define the moral being of the human individual. After all, his moral being does not refer only to the fact that man has a conscience, but also that man has the ability to decide whether or not he will act in conformity with his conscience. The conscience is not a mechanical gauge of quality; conscience is knowledge, it is a self-consciousness, but it is also a voice, a force which we can set aside and which we can counteract. We are able to silence the warning voice of conscience, we can disregard the approval of conscience; we can ridicule accusing conscience; in short, we can choose our position with respect to the conscience. Thus we are moral beings in two respects: we are moral, because we have a conscience; and we are moral, because we must make decisions respecting the voice of conscience.

Now by nature conscience itself is exclusively formal. It is no more than a self-consciousness that there is good and that there is evil; and that all the actions, all the deeds, which are subject to our willing come under the verdict of good or bad. The awareness of what is good and what is evil the conscience has received elsewhere. It may come from the general revelation of God, or from his special revelation; it may be derived from experience, it may be secured through education, or it may come from insight gained in some other way; but always the content of conscience is determined by that which it has received from elsewhere. By virtue of its nature, the content of conscience consists in norms which have taken possession of that conscience. It is a matter of the individual having been "captivated" by certain spiritual values; and in the gradual process of education, or perhaps along the stormy path of life's experience, the individual has learned to bow to the norms which have become the rulers of his conscience. This is a question of personality.

But we repeat: the human being retains the power to say "no" to his own conscience. This can be carried to such an extent that he finally completely silences the conscience. Hence the biblical expression that the conscience may be "seared as with a hot iron." Although it is a painful process, conscience may in the end be completely paralyzed and for all practical purposes cease to function. Now, the question as to how someone answers the voice of his conscience is a question of character.

It will be realized that in this way we receive some directions for steering a course in moral training. In brief: we are confronted with the problem of forming the conscience. But the forming of the conscience may largely be referred back to the forming of personality. Indeed, the question of the norms adopted by the individual in his conscience is related to the further question of which forces, which norms he recognizes as a human being; before which rulers does he bow? And this in turn is related to his religious life. The question is in which direction does he wish to serve; for religion is, viewed subjectively, primarily service.

If we bear in mind that the norm for moral life is given in the law of God, then we shall have to face the question how this obedience to the law of God must be viewed in the pedagogical relationships.

Obedience to the law must, after all, be an obedience in love. The ideal which we posit in our moral training is that the children may learn to love the law of God. "How love I Thy law, it is my meditation all the day." Our children must learn to obey that law, not out of legalism or out of fear, but because they experience that the law is good. And above all, our children will have to learn to obey, because they love God who has given the law. Love toward God must be the basis of moral behavior.

So far there are few difficulties.

But once we have ascertained this, questions arise; questions which, it is true, are related to practice, but which involve very important theoretical considerations. A number of these questions we wish to formulate.

Is it not wrong to demand obedience of the child, if the child is unable to be obedient to the law of God out of love? Is not the obedience manifested under such circumstances wholly immoral? Is it not the obedience of a slave who is compelled to do what the master says? Moreover, do we not teach our children to be hypocritical in this manner? After all, we say to the child: you must obey out of love. But let us assume the child also knows: "Whether I do it out of love or not, I must still obey." Will the final outcome then not be that the child feigns love just to be rid of the whole matter? And would it not be better simply to let the child have his way, when he does not desire to obey? At least we then know that the child is not making false pretenses. He does not know what real obedience is anyway, because he does not possess love.

To all appearances there is a very strict logic in this argument. However, we frequently observe that the persons who employ this logical weapon so masterfully do not usually act in complete accordance with the theory in the practice of their pedagogical activities. To all intents, this point of view eliminates all education. It would be consistent to state: whoever loves the law of God will do it anyway, and whoever does not love the law of God obeys in a wrong manner. The conclusion follows that we no longer have to educate, nor do we ever have to give any guidance to the child. For all practical purposes we have been relieved of our pedagogical responsibility. Let no one say that such reasoning reduces this viewpoint to absurdity. We have done nothing more than to apply this point of view in a practical way. And that has demonstrated the logical conclusion of this view.

What is really happening? It is possible to absolutize the proposition that man must obey the law of God out of love; and in the foregoing argument that has been done so rigorously that the real intent of the argument has been lost. Indeed, the proposition that we should obey the law of God out of love is a statement of an ideal, as is very evident from the words "should obey." Now it is a peculiarity of ideals that as a rule they do not describe the apex, if you will, the end of a path of development. The ideal is something which we pursue, which we attempt to lay hold on, and which, under favorable circumstances, we may sometimes attain. The depiction of the ideal, therefore, describes the result of a process or evolution. But the nature of ideals then also implies that we cannot regard the ideal as being in "absolute antithesis" to anything which does not fully approach the ideal. Indeed, the way to the ideal is a climbing path, in which each successive point attained by the climber approaches somewhat more closely the end-point, the apex of the ideal. The dynamic of striving toward the ideal would be foolish if we could only say: whoever has not attained to the ideal only does things which are sinful. Note the statement of Paul: "Not that I have already obtained, or am already made perfect: but I press on, if so be that I may lay hold on that for which also I was laid hold on by Christ Jesus" (Phil. 3: 12). When Paul states this, he depicts the man who is climbing on the pathway toward the ideal. Therefore it is wrong to state: since you have not attained the ideal, it is also better not to attempt to climb any longer; just turn about, or transfer to another path, for you are going in a direction opposite from that of the ideal.

Perfect obedience out of love is an ideal which people seldom comprehend. "Even the most holy men, while in this life, have only a small beginning of this obedience" (Heidelberg Catechism, Question 14). That is to say that the proposition defended in question-form above and stating that "in our training we do best to permit the children who do not obey out of love to do as they please," is therefore quite untenable. The proposition formulates the error made by those who do not understand the nature of the ideal as the positing of an ideal goal.

Furthermore, we observe in this connection that obedience in its ideal form must be gained or won; but then there are also steps in that obedience, that is, a lesser and greater attainment of the ideal; that is, standing farther from or nearer the ideal of obedience, but still within the frame-work of obedience. Whenever anyone obeys the law, that means that the law is effective in this concrete case, in this segment of life, and in itself that obedience is to the honor of God.

If the last statement is denied, then one will also have to deny that God will be glorified in the obedience which his enemies shall be compelled to render him ultimately. And yet that is precisely the majesty of God that one day "every knee shall be bowed and every tongue shall bless him" (Isa. 45). Obedience which is not purely out of love, because of the inadequacy of that love and because fears are present in one form or another, nevertheless has value, because God can be glorified in and by it.

But it also has value because it can and will have a pedagogical effect in teaching us the meaning of obedience. Repeatedly we shall experience, and the child, the young person will experience, that love is expressed in the commandment, in the law of God. The love of God toward us is expressed there and the love of God toward all of life. This insight is obtained only in the way of obedience. The way of obedience is God's way. The demand of Scripture is: "bend the twig while it is young"; "remember thy creator in the days of thy youth."

In the argument which we have rejected there is a misunderstanding not only with respect to the meaning of the ideal posited and the meaning of obedience, but there is also a misunderstanding about the nature of the law. In contrast to their Lutheran colleagues, Reformed theologians have always asserted that the law is the expression of the will of God; that the will of God and his essence are inseparable; that the law of God therefore is given with the being of God; and that accordingly the law of God holds, remains under all circumstances, and not only in time, but also in eternity; the law is not only for sinners upon earth, but also for the believers here upon earth and for the redeemed in heaven. The freedom from the law in which the believers glory is a freedom from the fear of the law, from the punishment of the law, from the oppressiveness of the law upon the life of the sinner. And it is due to this liberation that the law is regarded as glorious, as good.

It is only because the law is good and glorious, and because the real *usus normativus* is found again in this use of the law by the redeemed, that we must submit ourselves to that law in obedience. And therefore that law holds also for our life, whether we like it or not. To the same extent that we wish to resist the law, the law takes on its punitive character, its oppressive character. But then we shall also have to teach that disciplinary, oppressive, punitive character of the law so that our children may learn that the flesh is rebellion against the law, that it therefore resists God; thus they may also learn to ask for obedience out of love, in order that they may again serve God in the right manner. In this petition which prays for obedience out of love, there quite naturally should be included a confession of guilt for the fact that we resist the will of God; this confession of guilt is evoked by the law, which, as a taskmaster, impels us to Christ. And in Christ we then find the law in its wonderful character as an expression of both the essence and the love of God.

Thus we see that there can be no question of just "letting the child go its own way," when he is not obeying out of love. On the one hand this would mean that we would be depriving the child of the opportunity of coming to the recognition of the love which is implicit in the law; on the other hand, it would also mean that we deprive the law of its own character and that we would not be rendering God the honor which is due Him.

Therefore our conclusion is also: children who do not obey out of love and who resist obedience to the law must be compelled to obedience for the sake of God and for their own sake.

If the question is now raised as to what we can do for the forming of personality, then a further observation is necessary: we can only influence a personality significantly if its character is such that we can assume the possibility of that personality being influenced. Persons with various extremes in their character structure are practically ineducable as far as their personality is concerned. Children who are extremely servile, debilitated, indolent, hysterical, passive, purposeless, with little native ability, and with a tendency toward extreme extroversion, are so little subject to influence from without that we can hardly say that we are consciously engaged in the forming of their personality. Obviously, the environment will do something here, also for the forming of personality, but one is hardly able to speak in such instances of a deliberate and successful influencing of the personality.

From this single illustration it follows that the structure of the character of the child is of great significance for the question as to whether or not we can form the child into a personality. Certainly it is not true that every indivdual can be formed into a personality. For many persons integration and regulation of the personality cannot be brought about, due to the quality of inherited capacities. In addition it is possible that due to all kinds of external circumstances, the personality has already been influenced to such an extent that it is in fact no longer possible to speak of forming the personality. What is tragic about this situation is the fact that it may be present not only in decidedly abnormal individuals, but also in various young persons who are regarded as "normal" in society.

However, if we give our attention to a normal case of an educable personality, the question arises: how can we influence the forming of that personality? That question is indeed one of the most basic questions of pedagogics. In seeking an answer to the question, we should not overlook a fact, observed repeatedly by us already, namely, that personality and character belong together and that personality and character formation are essentially one. It can never be said that at one moment we are concerned with forming the personality and at another moment with the forming of character. The educator attempts to form his pupil into an individual who is a definite personality with a definite character.

Whenever we are educating, we are dealing with the total personality of the child. To be sure, our educational measures will at one time affect one area more, and at another time another area, but that does not imply that we are able to figure out even for a moment in which area our educational measures will have the greatest influence.

Of course it is true that a story which bears on some area of moral life may possibly influence the forming of the moral basis of character and simultaneously have significance for the forming of conscience as a part of personality. Indeed, that may be the case. The pedagogue therefore declares: If I tell story X and I do it well, then I know that by so doing, I am engaged in forming the moral personality, *in casu* the conscience, and at the same time I am influencing the moral basis of character. Now if such a conclusion were correct, then the question of education would be much more simple than it really is.

Let us assume that you have been able to ascertain the result mentioned above in a child for four or five times. This is, we may say, really a strange assumption, for as a rule one observes so few immediate concrete results from educational measures. However, it is still possible that the sixth time you will suddenly discover that, by your story, you have had a very detrimental influence upon the child, and that the expression of his character has been adversely affected. Because of the story the child has developed such great fear that he is not able to act purposively. He is compelled to assume an attitude of passivity. And the child who was previously somewhat "psychasthenic" has developed the feeling of never being able to measure up to the goal set before it. This is merely an example. Everyone will understand that in practice there are innumerable possibilities in which the reaction to our pedagogical measures may be quite different from what we had anticipated.

If we consider all these facts, then we get the impression that the possibilities of purposive personality forming and character forming are extremely meager. However, it would be presumptuous to draw such a conclusion at this point. From what has been said thus far, we can only conclude that the influence we can bring to bear on the forming of personality and character does not follow such straight lines as some statements might lead one to think.

At the same time, we should not overlook the great significance of the milieu, of the group, in the forming of the personality and character of the child. A class-room can contribute much, and a youth organization even more to the proper forming of the child's personality. But everyone will understand that the group which is of greatest importance is the one to which the child belongs by nature, that is, the family.

Naturally, this does not imply that every family, as it is in our time, constitutes an ideal basis for personality-forming. On the contrary. Here, too, many complaints may be heard. Unfortunately, there are all too many broken homes, families with unbalanced parents; there are too many families in which materialism, egoism, and egocentrism dominate. We have already commented on the fact that there can be no forming of the personality and character of children in such families. The basic feature of personality and character forming is the shaping of individuals who control themselves; that is, persons whose ego is master in the microcosmos of their own psychical existence; people who in the most absolute sense are subject to the norms which they acknowledge; and therefore also human beings who assume and experience norms, seeking a harmonious balance between the extremes of life. And in particular, they seek the harmonious balance which fits their own personality and native capacity. Now then, such an equilibrium and such a respectful acknowledgement of accepted norms comes into being only in a milieu in which norms are accepted and lived in a balanced way. The disease which has infected homes in our time is also the malady by which the forming of personality and character is constantly threatened in this day and age.

For the sake of brevity may I be permitted to circumscribe now the points which are of greatest significance for the forming of the child's personality and character within the family.

Education in the family must constantly be directed toward giving the child no more and no less responsibility than he is able to bear. From earliest youth the child himself should do whatever he is capable of doing. As early as possible he should learn to dress himself, to polish his own shoes, to care for his own school-books, and to keep his own room tidy, even though mother does the dusting and makes the bed. The little child who plays should put away his own toys. In brief, from the outset the child should learn to be responsible for his own things.

In the second place, the child should learn to control his own "appetite" in earliest childhood. The child has to eat what mother gives him. The child must learn to govern his passions. In addition, there must be rule and regulation in the life of the child, although not enforced of course. The child must get up and go to bed on time without whining and whimpering. We conclude: self-control and submission to rules, in a word: obedience is the first and best means of forming the personality.

A third important factor is for the parents to teach the child that they themselves also exercise obedience. The parents must daily cause the child to experience the fact of their obedience to the will of God. In this way the child learns to be respectful of norms and thus the conscience of the child is being formed.

And for the sake of forming the personality and character of their child, it is necessary, in the fourth place, that the parents treat the child according to his age and nature in the training process. The object of all discipline is to bring the child to self-discipline. The purpose of all guidance is to teach the child to walk alone. For that reason the habits of some parents are so terrible. This is true especially of some mothers, who out of fear take every possible precaution for the child, making as it were a girdle of cares about the child. The result is that the child never learns to see out of his own eyes or to stand on his own feet. A reasonably intelligent child should learn to walk in the street alone. The purpose of moral training is further to teach the child to walk alone morally. A child who from his first to his eighteenth year is surrounded by prohibitions and admonitions will never become a personality. The child must himself know what he may do, and what is the measure befitting his age. In addition, the child must learn to refrain from what is wrong out of love for the norms and the law. But what is more, the child should be taught to do that which is right and good. Only in this way will the conscience be exercised.

It need hardly be added that a good personal contact between teacher and pupil is of the greatest importance. Wisdom, which is the most precious gift of God in life, must in the final analysis also be the principal ideal in the forming of personalities and characters. The verdict of a Solomon is ingenious, a fruit of wisdom, even though you may reason the logic of it after the event. The Scriptures do not call Solomon intelligent or clever, or even a great thinker, but they speak of him as being wise!

Now then, this wisdom cannot be taught. It is a possession. And this wisdom is the source of the ingeniousness, and is the basis for judgment.

It is understandable that modern psychology has so little to say about wisdom. Wisdom cannot be analyzed. Perhaps it may be tested, but it is exceedingly difficult to develop purposively in training. Usually we can only ascertain whether or not it is present. And it is present so little in life.

That wisdom is a matter of a life's attitude in the first place. There is an atmosphere in which wisdom cannot flourish. And fortunately, there is also an atmosphere in which wisdom can grow.

And the fear of the Lord is the beginning of wisdom.

5

Cultural Forming and Christian Education

WHENEVER we speak of the subject, *cultural forming* we are dealing with an extremely difficult problem. There is, as you know, still comparatively little agreement in Christian circles as to what constitutes the essence of culture. Consequently, if we speak of cultural forming and Christian education, we must determine what we *mean* by cultural forming; and even prior to discussing cultural forming we shall have to state our views on culture. Needless to say, our attempt to get at the essence of culture is based on Revelation. At the outset I wish to state that, from the very nature of the case, it would be possible to speak much more extensively on this subject than I shall be able to do in this lecture. I shall be able only to draw a few basic lines, thereby limiting myself to that which is most essential to my subject. It will become evident that occasionally I am critical of the terminology which is customarily employed. My criticism relates primarily to terminology, to the manner of expression, rather than to the intent of those expressions; although it will also become evident that on occasion I do not share the opinions of others who speak or write on these matters.

And if hereafter I state, for example, that the *term* "Christian Learning" (science, philosophy) is open to dispute, then every well-meaning listener will understand at once that I certainly have no intention of combatting Christian scholarship and research as practised up to this time. To put it very concretely: I would not call into question for a moment the rightful place of a Christian university; on the contrary, I should be prepared, if necessary, to fight for the existence of such a university every hour of my life. I state this as emphatically and as expressly as possible, even at the risk of sounding emotional, to avoid all possibility of misunderstanding. However, I am also convinced that, particularly with respect to such concepts as "Christian science," "Christian art," and the like, an uncritical usage has developed in Calvinistic circles; that is, these terms are constantly being used without due consideration of their exact meaning. But precisely for this reason it is all the more necessary to reflect on our terminology and to consider the meaning of our words.

From a historical point of view, the development of such terms as "Christian culture," "Christian art," "Christian science," and the like, is fully understandable. And I am sure everyone will believe me when I state that I am in full sympathy with what is commonly understood and implied by those terms. However, that does not take away the possibility that one may consider it necessary to posit the inaccuracy of such terminology; and the more so, if this will enable him to define more readily the view which in his judgment is Scriptural and therefore correct in principle.

As a preliminary to my further discussion, I deem it necessary, secondly, to state what I mean by culture, by art, and by science (scientific scholarship). I shall attempt to refrain from giving a definition. Definitions in this area are dangerous. As you know, every definition is a definition only if that which is defined can be subordinated to a higher concept. Any idea which is wholly peculiar, and which relates to a matter which is unique in kind, cannot possibly be defined therefore. Culture is unique in kind, and hence it cannot be given an exact scientific definition. We can, however, attempt to circumscribe what we mean by culture and I am willing to undertake that.

Needless to say, I shall also then be touching upon the concepts of culture, art, and science. Although art and science are constituent parts of culture, yet they must sometimes be mentioned separately, if only for the reason that it is possible to clarify the meaning better by one of these two than by the general concept of culture.

Culture is used in a two-fold sense. I may view "culture" as an activity, or as the product of that activity. As an activity, culture is that formative action of man whereby he transforms some native capacity or natural resource in such a manner that his fellow man is able to experience, appreciate, or enjoy it to the glory of Him who gave it.

Culture as "culture-acquisition" is already the result of such an action. Thus the goal of culture is to reveal the gifts of creation, but in such a form that God is glorified and human life enriched by it. Not all gifts of nature require a "cultural" form before they can be experienced, appreciated, or enjoyed by man. Water is not a product of culture, but we quench our thirst with it. Nor are the outstretched plains a product of culture, though under favorable circumstances we can enjoy their beauty. Nevertheless, bread is the product of a cultural activity, and precisely in this form do we enjoy the gift of nature which is given to us in the grain.

Matters are somewhat different with respect to art. The significance of art is always the experiencing of beauty. Man can no more create the basis for culture himself than he can create beauty, for the basis of man's cultural activity must always be found in creation itself; and the experience of beauty, therefore, will always have to be founded in the beauty which God has given in his creation. Thus true art always has as its final end the enjoyment of God-given beauty. In the world the beautiful and the non-beautiful can exist side by side in the same object; the latter may even contribute to the former, although not-beauty then participates in beauty. A discordant note may be required to accentuate a harmony.

We are living in a sinful world and for that reason we are confronted with tremendous problems, also in the area of culture and art; of these we shall speak in greater detail presently.

By science we do not mean simply knowledge. The knowledge of many facts, "being well informed," does not necessarily have anything to do with science or systematized learning. Knowing is always related to the Greek word *phidein*: that is to say, one sees, has insight, penetrates things; one sees things in relationship. Science seeks answers to the "why" and "how" of things; science searches for the foundations of things; it seeks out the relationships which exist.

Now to be able to engage in scientific studies it is positively necessary to possess knowledge. One cannot see the relationships between things without knowing the things themselves. For that matter, the thing itself is as a rule a combination of other things and the relations between those things.

However, the moment you say "relationship" or "relation" you also state "the point of view from which you determine that relation." Accordingly, it is inconceivable that any scientific activity can take place without a pre- or extra-scientific principle. It will be recalled that we have dealt with this matter before.

In our judgment, the only possibility of really seeing the relations of things, of gaining something of a true insight, will depend upon our observation of the light of God's revelation over life and our seeing things in the light of that revelation of God. The idea advocated here has such force that he who has little knowledge of facts and who, in general, is not scientifically formed, but walks in the light of the Word of God, nevertheless has a more penetrating and truer insight into life's relationships than the renowned scientific scholar who possesses great erudition, but who does not know the Source of knowledge and who does not comprehend the statement: "In Thy Light we see the Light."

But with this outlook, also, a great many questions remain.

The Calvinistic life and world view, having encountered the problem of nature and grace in the Roman Catholic view of life, has wrestled with this problem repeatedly.

On the one hand it is true that the entire creation is under the curse because of man. On the other hand it is also true that God gives a treasury of blessings to the whole life of man. Out of this seeming contradiction all kinds of problems gradually emerge. The question of common grace, which has come up repeatedly in various Reformed circles during the past half century, is related to this problem.

However, now we are dealing with the nature of culture. We repeat: culture is to reveal or manifest the gifts of creation in such a form that God is exalted and human life is enriched. But now we must face the question: to what extent are the products of culture sinful?

In speaking of this problem, we may commence by observing that many people have a wrong concept of the essence of sin. Frequently sin is regarded almost as something material, as something that adheres in the "thing." Now that view is wrong. Sin is never "something," a thing, matter, material, or what have you. Sin is negative.* Sin is a lack, a privation, the absence of something. Sin is the absence of righteousness. Therefore, only that can be sinful which has a moral status; that which can possess righteousness. A tree, a plank, a knife, a revolver, cannot lack righteousness. Neither is an animal a moral creature; hence it has no righteousness and cannot be said to "lack righteousness." Man only is a moral creature.

* This is not to be construed in the sense of "passive."

He is created after the image of God and he alone can possess righteousness or lack righteousness.

From this follows the principle that no thing, object, work of art, or weapon can be sinful. No thing ever has sin. But man can indeed be sinful and man can use a thing in a sinful way. When a surgeon uses his knife to perform surgery on a patient, he performs an act which is justified and one which is not without righteousness, since he is fulfilling his duty as a surgeon. But if in a fit of anger he seizes that knife to stab someone with it, then he is using that same knife, and he is the same man, but his deed is sinful. The knife remains the same. But we shall have to develop this thought even further. Let us assume that I see a man some distance away striking a boy with a stick. I do not know if the man is sinning; that depends upon the motivation of the man who is wielding the stick. I cannot say whether that striking is good or bad in itself. If I assume the man is hitting back in self-defense at a young man who has attacked him, and if I leave out of consideration any secondary motivations, then it must be said that the attitude of his man's heart in this simple act of self-defense is a good one; the man's striking with the stick is also righteous and he is not sinning. And if the man should happen to be a father who is inflicting legitimate punishment upon his son, then he likewise is not sinning. But if it should turn out to be a man who in a hot temper is beating his neighbor, then he certainly is sinning.

Consequently, we should understand clearly that in judging the use of a thing, whatever that thing may be, we are always concerned with the attitude, the disposition of the heart. The heart of man is ever central, or as we say, "the heart of the matter."

Thus the dance-floor is not sinful. The individual who walks over a dance-floor is not necessarily sinning. Even the man who is dancing on the dance-floor may not be sinning. It depends upon the predisposition of his heart while he is dancing. If this man, while dancing, rejoices in the gift which he has received from his Creator, then that man does not sin. But if passions begin to stir within his heart, because again and again he experiences physical contact with his partner, then he may be sinning indeed.

We now touch upon a point to which we shall return presently, namely, the question of using things in such a way that we are easily led into wrong actions. Matches are not sinful things, and it is quite all right to strike a match. But a child who plays with matches on a haystack is doing wrong. It is so easy for the child to set the haystack on fire. People who are dancing on a dance-floor are in many respects like children who are playing with matches on a haystack.

Thus we now have the proposition that sin dwells in the heart of man and no thing is ever sinful, and we can only say that the manner in which men use things is sinful.

We are now confronted with a second problem: the question of the nature or essence of culture and cultural life.

What is culture? Well, culture is always the fruit of creation. That must be our starting point. There is no culture which does not have its birth in nature. Just as the man who is engaged in economic activities can create nothing new in the economic process, so the man who is engaged in culture can really create nothing new in culture. All he can do is to discover that which is present as creational reality; and he can work or form this material of creation in such a way that he obtains results which may be designated as culture-acquisitions. When Rembrandt was painting his *Night-Watch* he was producing a tremendously valuable culture-product. But Rembrandt received his talent as a gift of creation. Let us assume for a moment that Rembrandt had lived in a world in which the art of painting was wholly unknown, in which there was no cloth, no paint, no pallette; then Rembrandt would not have become a painter. And even if Rembrandt had lived in a world of painters, but himself had been lacking in the talent to paint, he would never have made the *Night-Watch*. It could be painted only because the conditions were favorable, through the coincidence, concurrence, and conjunction of the various gifts of God's creation: Rembrandt's talents as a painter, the status of technological development in the making of paints and canvases, and the like. The conjunction of these creation-gifts in a person at a given time with that given talent and life's development, made it possible for the *Night-Watch* to be created.

Accordingly, we speak of creative artists; but "to create" in this connection has a special meaning, that is, to produce something which did not previously exist as the thing or object it has now become. "To be a creative artist" does not mean, however, that the artist-creator is able to take even a single element not previously existent in creation and use it for, add it to, or demonstrate it in his work. Therefore all culture-products are the creation of God. Every product of culture comes from God and it must also serve God.

Since this is true, no product of culture can be sinful in itself. This does not imply, of course, that people are not able to *use* some specific culture-product in a sinful manner. The copper serpent which was raised in the wilderness at the command of God was used in a sinful manner later, and therefore it had to be destroyed. But that did not make the copper snake itself a sinful object. The people had made sinful use of it; and thus in this instance too, the sin was in the hearts of the people.

From the Scriptures it is evident how little the thing itself determines its holiness or unholiness. How should I look upon the vessels in the temple at Jerusalem? First they were in the temple and later they were pillaged by Nebuchadnezzar (II Chron. 36:18). In Babylon they were used at the carousals of the king (Dan. 5:2, 3). And thereafter Ezra again took them back for the new temple (Ezra 1).

Perhaps someone will say: "Yes, but those vessels were made for a holy purpose." May I be permitted to point out that David received and plundered all kinds of vessels from his enemies (II Sam. 8:10-12). Without a doubt those vessels had fulfilled a function in the pagan culture. Yet David dedicates them to the Lord and Solomon places them in the temple (I Kings 7:51).

However, the objection might be raised that after all this was not according to the will of the Lord. But that objection is set aside by what we read in Numbers 31. There we read that the Lord demands of Moses that he take from the treasures of the Midianites golden vessels which are to remain in the tabernacle. They were all finely wrought vessels which were taken from the Midianites and which were placed before the countenance of the Lord. Now would anyone really be able to insist that these vessels were a foreign element among the treasures of the house of the Lord? I believe that we should not approach these matters from a theoretical point of view, but rather that our thinking should be oriented to the Scriptures; and then, in my judgment, little remains of the theory of the function of an idol in a degenerate culture.

What is the fallacy in such an argumentation? It is this: no distinction is made between the cultural activity of the unregenerate man and the product of his activity, the thing made; the characteristics of the acting individual are projected into, are attributed to, the resulting object. This logical leap is not justifiable.

However, the question then remains: Is it not possible for an artist to so express his sinful inclinations in a work of art that others are easily led to sin? And if the question is stated thus, we shall doubtlessly answer it in the affirmative. If a talented individual—whether he is really an artist is still another matter—paints an obscene picture which can excite passionate lusts especially in young people, then that obscenity has been so strongly expressed in the picture that we condemn the picture itself. Yet we do not say: the picture is sinful. However, there is in it so much of the painter's wantonness that it readily brings others to sin because it plays upon the sinful heart of man. Such products of so-called art are to be unhesitatingly condemned.

This quite naturally confronts us with still another problem. That problem is: are we now also able to say that the obscene picture, this product of culture, contains only that which was previously existent in creation? Apparently we are touching upon a difficult problem at this point; we are here dealing with a question which, particularly in Christian circles, has led to all kinds of misunderstanding with respect to art and the products of culture.

The following elements make up the problem:

a. A person produces a cultural object.

b. This individual "informs" this product of culture with his whole being, his entire personality, his emotion.

c. If the culture-product is a "success," it will give expression to that which moved the maker.

d. The individual who enjoys this product of culture relives, at least in part, something of the experience of the maker.

e. The culture-product therefore stimulates in man certain sensations of which he can have an esthetic awareness.

Now in these instances we are dealing exclusively with persons whose nature is sinful. It is conceivable that the maker of the art-product, whether intentional or otherwise, expresses something which lacks righteousness, and which is therefore sinful, in his work of art. It is also possible that the artist has wrought his art frankly, honestly, and simply in an adoring veneration of the beauty of God's creation. If the artist is truly great, then this difference in the work of art will be evident to the individual with fine sensibility and esthetic appreciation.

But the persons who observe the work of art are also sinful. Because of their own perversity, or because of their extreme sensitivity in one direction or another, they may see something in the work of art which is not really there. Vice versa, it could be that the artist had more or less intentionally desired to express some wantonness in his work of art, but that others who view the art-product experience only the beauty without observing its "wanton" features.

Everyone senses how many problems can arise in this area. For certain individuals a perfectly innocent depiction may arouse wrong sensations. The response of other individuals to an impure picture may be wholly pure and sound. To all appearances we do not possess a single objective criterion; perhaps we should conclude: it is best to banish from art all that which may stimulate wrong excitations in certain individuals. However, these are mere appearances and not true. We should not overlook the fact that some sensitive persons may be excited by all possible kinds of objects. A man may receive a wrong stimulus from seeing the seams of a lady's stocking, or from catching sight of the lingerie beneath her dress. Obviously we cannot say that women ought not to go swimming because some perverted men have lustful sensations when they see a woman in a bathing suit. The fact of the matter is that we should not seek the criterion of an object in the misuse to which it is put by some persons; but our criterion should be determined rather by the intent of the artist, by the nature of the work of art, and by the soul of the artist. In this manner the work of art becomes its own criterion. If a given cultural product is ethically acceptable in the judgment and feeling of experienced critics of high, moral, Christian standing, then the art-product as such must be accepted, and any misuse which individuals with a perverse nature make of it is the responsibility of those perverted individuals.

Conversely, if a so-called art product manifestly reveals something of the sinful and perverse inclinations of the artist, then that "art product" should no longer be reckoned among the acquisitions of culture. I am aware that it is difficult to make exact demarcations at this point. Dubious cases will always remain; but that is true in every field.

It stands to reason that the view discussed above holds not only for the tactual but also for the auditory products of culture. The question of the culture-value of hot jazz and swing must be decided by criteria such as we have outlined. Since these so-called musical expressions play on sentiment and vegetate on nervous fatigue, they constitute a permanent negative stimulus to the human nervous system, even though it may be true that some persons react to these stimuli with shivering pleasure. For us Occidentals, therefore, these so-called musical expressions cannot be classified as acceptable culture.

We must now ask the question to what extent we are able to speak of Christian culture-products and Christian works of art. Is Rembrandt's *Night-Watch* a Christian painting or not?

Permit me to begin by stating that I cannot accept such a formulation of the problem. Whether or not a person is Christian will depend on whether or not he acknowledges Christ as King of his life. But a "thing" can never be Christian. After all, a thing has no ethical determination. Therefore, I do not wish to speak of Christian culture. There is either culture or a lack of culture. Everything that is true culture may be included within the meaning of Christian culture, as that term is used by some persons. The question may then be raised: Is there then no pagan culture, and should we not place in opposition to the idea of a pagan culture that of a Christian culture? If such a question were raised in a public gathering, the crowd would at once take this to mean defeat for the proponent of the idea that no Christian culture exists or can exist. And I am aware that there is a certain preference for the phrase "Christian culture" in circles which provide leadership in Christian thinking, so that they too will accept the argument derived from the term "pagan culture." Permit me to state that I desire nevertheless to maintain the thesis that in the strict sense of the word we cannot speak of "Christian culture."

As I have stated previously, the word culture may be related to two things: first, to the activity of creating culture, that is, being active in a cultural way; and second, to the product of that cultural activity. In the former instance there of course can be no question of Christian culture, but at best we can speak of the cultural activity of a Christian. And in the latter instance I am always concerned with a thing. Thus when we speak of pagan culture, the product of this so-called pagan culture may not be described as being "pagan." For the thing itself is neither Christian nor pagan. It is a thing and therefore it cannot be given an ethical or a religious qualification. Now there remain two possibilities: on the one hand that product of pagan culture may clearly manifest certain sinful tendencies in human life, in which case it is not culture, but the opposite of culture, like the product of the dissolute painter; on the other hand the product of the pagan culture-creator is—like the *Night-Watch* of Rembrandt—wholly the result of the creative talent which God has placed in the cosmos, and then it is culture, and nothing but culture.

Accordingly, we state that all "culture-products" in the world fall within the classification: "culture" or "non-culture." As soon as culture and the acquisitions of culture manifest something of man's sinful nature, in the sense that it becomes very evident that the maker of the culture-product lacked that righteousness and truth which is revealed in all of God's works, then we are no longer dealing with a genuine product of culture. Whether the maker is a pagan or a Christian makes no difference at all.

Now we shall have to distinguish carefully. It is possible for an artist to portray that which is sinful without his work of art becoming non-culture. It all depends on how one describes, draws, or depicts that sin. The question is not one of whether we may paint the episode of Lot and his daughters, but it is a question of how we paint that scene. Neither is it a question of whether some perverse natures may be stimulated in the wrong way by such a painting, but the question is one of what the artist truly expresses, as that is regarded in the judgment of qualified esthetic critics. And, we should add, in the judgment of those qualified critics who apply the right criteria.

The Boeroeboedoer temple on Java certainly was not built by Christians, but it is a tremendous cultural acquisition. In spite of the fact that pagans erected this culture-monument, there is nothing in it which plays on the sinful nature of man. Even the depiction of idols in such monuments of culture is not in itself justification for condemning the monument. After all, the monument itself is not the veneration of an idol. In the monument itself we have a beautiful image, which has come from the imagination of the maker. That imagination, it must be granted, has a very definite religious orientation. And besides this: "An idol is nothing."

Furthermore, if those who speak of "Christian culture" are consistent, they will have to draw several exceedingly awkward and difficult conclusions. For "culture" is not only the totality of all art products, but "culture" includes also the field which is cultivated with rye or wheat or potatoes. The field of grass lying like a green mat between the other cultivated fields is also "culture." Now if you are going to be consistent in speaking of Christian and non-Christian culture, you will have to extend the line of demarcation and conclude that a field may be cultivated in both a Christian and a non-Christian manner. Obviously, the person cultivating may be a Christian or a non-Christian, but that is another matter. The difference in the art of cultivation can only be one of genuine or non-genuine culture; a difference of more or less culture. Should anyone wish to speak of land cultivated in a Christian manner and land cultivated in a non-Christian manner, he will experience great difficulty in finding a point where he can suddenly distinguish between Christian and non-Christian culture. All our daily utensils, all our furniture, all our dinner-service is the product of culture and hence it is culture-acquisition. I cannot imagine that anyone is able to speak of Christian and non-Christian cups and saucers.

Now we shall proceed a step further. Let us take, for example, handmade cups, the graceful product of the art of pottery. One cannot make the above distinction according to types here either. Let us assume further that the cup becomes a bowl, and the bowl a vase. Where does the distinction Christian and non-Christian now begin? And from the vase you may proceed to the sculptured vase, to sculpture, to painting and so on.

From this argument too it becomes clear that we are not able to speak of Christian culture. Of course this does not mean to say that we cannot speak of the culture of Christians. However, we can also speak of the shoes of Christians, the watches of Christians. But that obviously has nothing to do with the matter we are discussing. Indeed, the culture-product of a Christian may in itself be non-culture.

In the use of the term "Christian culture" there is, in my opinion, a wholly unmotivated capitulation of Christianity to humanism and paganism. To speak of "Christian culture, art and science" is to admit by implication that what is designated as "non-Christian culture, art, and science," is also genuine culture, art, and science. This capitulation I refuse to make. The so-called non-Christian sciences contain elements of knowledge only insofar as they are in agreement with the truth; but those elements in the sciences which agree with the truth, are elements belonging to the so-called "Christian sciences."

After what has been said here about Christian culture, Christian science, and Christian art, some individual may wish to ask if we then can speak of Christian education, Christian schools, Christian societies, Christian politics, and the like.

I can well imagine that such questions are raised. Yet without a doubt we shall have to continue speaking of Christian politics, Christian social action, Christian schools, and Christian education.

Now how is this to be explained and how is it to be reconciled with what we have stated previously? Let us examine what this question really is getting at. In culture, in art, in science the problem is one of reflecting, of reproducing something which is present in creation. I am able to know creation only in the light of the Scriptures and thus I arrive at the sciences, not "Christian sciences," but science in its own right.

Whether or not I have become familiar with culture, science, and art, I stand in a world in which I must act. This is a significant difference, for here I am concerned with objectives. I want to move in a certain direction. I want to change life. I want to do something about life. I want to obey the law of God in this life.

I engage in politics. That is to say, I want to exert influence upon the government. It is my desire to impel the government in a certain direction. Now if I should wish to move the government in the direction of communism, I should also engage in politics, but a definite kind of politics, politics which moves in a definite direction. And if I desire to impel the government in a positively Christian direction, then my political activity also will move in a definite direction. I cannot say: communistic politics is not politics, is non-politics; on the contrary, that is also politics, although I may regard those politics as wrong.

Politics therefore is quite different from science. Science which does not gain the truth, but achieves the lie, is not "wrong science," but it is non-science. Art which does not demonstrate the beauty of creation, but rather the baseness of the human heart, is not "wrong art," but it is non-art. For true art is always directed toward the creator. But in the area of politics things are different. Real politics always is directed towards the governing of the state, towards the polity of the government. Politics does not aim to realize the order of creation, but it aims to give a certain direction to the form of government. And as soon as I speak of a direction, I can say: "right," and "left," "upwards," and "downwards."

Everyone will realize that we are on wholly different territory now. Let us take another example. I am able to teach. In my teaching I do not aim to realize the order of creation. I aim to teach the child some knowledge and I intend to give direction to the life of the child. And no sooner do I speak of "direction" before the possibility exists of going in all directions.

But that also implies that when I speak of "schools," when I speak of "politics," when I speak of "social organization," I must also indicate the direction in which I want to go. For my attitude is ethically determined by definite principles upon which I act.

Therefore it is very definitely necessary to give an adjectival modifier when we speak of education, school, social action, politics, and the like.

Thus we see that the view which we defend most certainly maintains the antithesis in life. This antithesis becomes evident in every area in which man acts according to norms.

The question now before us is: Does an antithesis exist? Really this question should be: Does the antithesis exist?

This brings up the further question whether we must recognize the antithesis in the field of education, and whether we must regard this antithesis as being significant for the theory of pedagogy.

Before answering this question we must again call to mind an idea which we have emphasized repeatedly, namely, that pedagogy is a normative science. It deals with norms and it describes actions in compliance with those norms.

Now these norms are always rooted in a life and world view, irrespective of what that view is. The central question is whether we should look upon these norms as being equal in value, regardless of the spiritual climate, or regardless of the life and world view from which they stem.

Are the norms of the atheist of equal value with those of the deist, and do these in turn have the same value and significance as the norms of the theist? Are the norms derived from the Vedas on a par with those derived from the Bible? Do the norms posited by Jesus Christ have the same value and significance as the norms defined by Buddha, Confucius, or Stalin?

Now a life and world view which claims to be exclusive, sets itself up in contrast with all other views of life. Here one's own norms rule, and the norms of other outlooks on life are recognized only insofar as they are identical with our own views.

In consequence, every life and world view which claims truth as its characteristic is in antithesis to all other views of life in respect to both its own basic structure and the norms which it posits. This antithesis is related to the fact that every life and world view has the character of a confession of faith. A life and world view always dominates all of life.

When Christianity, therefore, comes with the argument that the Truth, that the Scripture itself, is the revelation of God and that God's revelation has become flesh in Jesus Christ, then this Christianity makes a decisive claim. Whatever is not in agreement with the truth is a lie. The revelation of God furnishes all of life with a guide-line. The norms which God gives are divine norms. God speaks with authority: "Thou shalt . . ."

By taking this position, Christianity formally makes no pretense of claiming anything other than that which every life and world view posits. And it may be useful to comment here that those persons who deny that the Scriptures impose such binding norms themselves furnish norms with an exclusive character for the interpretation of the Scriptures, and for their attitude toward the Word and the Gospel preaching.

Particularly in the field of pedagogy, where we constantly encounter normative problems, there is no alternative but to recognize the fact that from a formal, scientific point of view, a life and world view which by its very nature claims to be exclusive must stand in antithesis to every other view by which it is rejected.

Thus in any area where normative action is required, Christianity stands in antithesis to every other set of norms. Now this is not *an* antithesis; this is *the* antithesis. Indeed, does Christ not himself expressly state that He has come into the world for the sake of crisis? Christ is the sign which is spoken against; He is the downfall and the resurrection; He is the way, the truth, and the life.

And that therefore constitutes the antithesis. It is not made by man, but it is a fact which God himself posits in his Word; a fact, moreover, which the church of all ages has experienced as a fact, and which every Christian also observes in his heart each day.

This antithesis runs diagonally through all normative activity in the life of culture.

Therefore, pedagogy cannot avoid the choice: for or against Christ—to obey, or not to obey Him who is the King of life.

Now people who aim to be obedient to the God-given norms in their actions will continue to be persons with shortcomings. There can be differences of insight, therefore, among persons who want to be obedient to the norms of God. But fundamentally they are, nevertheless, in agreement.

Christian pedagogy should attempt to give expression to such a unity. And pedagogues throughout the world who desire to observe the God-given norms obediently will have to work together to come to agreement in the development of a pedagogy, and consequently also in the building of a culture which adapts itself to the God-given norms in faith and obedience.

The question now naturally arises: What do we mean when we state that there must be cultural training and that man must be able to conduct himself as a cultured individual within his culture?

In answering this question, we wish to point out first that in our opinion not every individual who participates in, lives in a culture, can legitimately be regarded as a "cultured individual." Certainly, the bar-tender who starts a brawl is not behaving like a "man of culture." Even though he may have a function in modern culture, as a pugnacious fellow, he manifests very little cultural habitude.

That we are able to make this distinction is due to the fact that in daily life the concepts "culture," "cultured individual" and "man of culture" are bandied about. It is very confusing to state that a bar-tender is a "man of modern culture" and to state simultaneously that a bar-keeper who engages in brawls is not behaving like a "man of culture." The word "modern culture" is used to designate the total complex of systems which we observe in societal life in different ways as a fruit of man's domination over nature. The man of culture is then an individual who performs a function in this society. But taken in the strict sense of the word this means that every individual is a "man of culture." Even the illiterate beggar may be a phenomenon of culture in a certain region of a country. He may "belong" to it, being a more or less integrated part of the structure of the local life.

But in speaking of culture and culture phenomena in this manner we are using the word "culture" in a very general sense. In this context it is difficult to find a substitute for the word "culture." Really we should speak of "the structure of corporate life;" or "societal structure." But in any case, when the word "culture" is used in this sense its meaning is quite different than when we are discussing "cultural education" or "cultural forming."

In the latter instance the word "culture" means "culture in a narrower sense"; we then think more narrowly of the potentialities of individuals to participate in the culture-process, and of the individual's sharing in the treasures of culture which a nation, or possibly even mankind, possesses.

These are, accordingly, two aspects. "Cultural forming" is "forming of the personality," in such a way that it is able to share in the general cultural heritage; it is also bringing the general acquisitions of culture to the individual so that he himself can develop cultural activities.

This sharing in the general cultural heritage demands a cultural forming which is broader than a mere "having access to art and science." It is true that the condition of a person's clothes is not strictly a matter of culture, but one of civilization, and one's finger-nails belong to nature rather than to "culture." Yet it is a matter of "cultural forming" whether a person wears a clean or a dirty collar; whether he picks up a book with neat finger-nails, or with nails which show a border of black. The fact is that there exists a somewhat vaguely defined quality which we designate as "cultural habitude." The vagueness of this description is related to the existence of individual variations which in turn produce variations in the possible form of this cultural habitude. There are persons who dress very neatly, and who are well-groomed to all outward appearances, who, nevertheless, do not possess "cultural habitude." There are others who dress very slovenly, and who are far from having a conventional attitude, but in whose every action, gesture, and appearance one can observe "the cultured individual."

This peculiar and yet typical phenomenon can, as a matter of fact, be observed and experienced only by persons who themselves have attained a certain cultural level. Thus the "peculiarity" which we call "cultural habitude" cannot possibly be described in a few sentences.

In any case it is remarkable that "cultural habitude" is always and very definitely a specific description of behavior. Characteristic features which are important, sometimes very important, in judging an individual's general classification, frequently have no significance for the question as to whether or not we attribute "cultural habitude" to a person.

The important thing for education is that this cultural habitude is instilled in the child by a process of transfer. The "attitude" in the home, the "attitude" of the teacher or instructor is of signal importance.

Naturally, this is by no means all that can be said on this subject. The acceptance of culture, as well as the ability to understand and appreciate culture, also presupposes affinity for culture. There must be a cultural interest. This interest is nurtured to a large extent by education, but it is also a question of aptitude.

Furthermore, this interest in culture and the ultimate accepance of culture is possible only where there is knowledge of culture and at least some insight into the meaning of culture.

Culture forming, therefore, is not conceivable unless the child or young person, under guidance, is brought into contact with the cultural heritage. The avenue of approach in making this contact will depend in part upon the aptitude of the young person. And at a later age the choice of a life's vocation will also be determinative of the direction in which cultural contacts are to be made.

Finally, we desire to call attention to a danger which should be avoided in the formulation of aims for cultural forming. We should acquaint the child with the cultural heritage on its own level, and not in terms of the insight and experience of adults. Unless we do this, the "acquaintance of the child with culture" all too readily becomes an intellectual approach to the problematics connected with a work of art. Whenever "acquaintance with culture" is restricted to the area of "knowing," it soon becomes a matter of schematic assimilation of certain facts without any deeper background contacts. Education in culture will have to consider seriously the question: to what extent are children and young people able to experience and appreciate cultural values?

In addition, pedagogy will have to give far more serious consideration than it has so far to the problem: what should be the order in which we present the acquisitions of culture to the child?

The question: What is cultural forming? remains still to be answered. I shall attempt to formulate as briefly as possible the answer to this question.

In essence culture means that the individual himself is wholly formed, as described in the lecture, "The Objectives of Christian Education." If this forming has been achieved in the right way, cultural forming has taken place. When an individual possessing certain given talents occupies a position in the cultural community and is capable of serving that cultural life with his native abilities, then cultural forming has taken place. In cultural forming there is, therefore, a strong emphasis upon the necessity of forming the whole personality with a view to every aspect of life.

However, we should not neglect to underscore carefully one matter. The culturally formed individual should be able to live at least on that level of culture which in his time is accepted as "the mean level of culture." This concept, "the mean level of culture," is difficult to circumscribe. I should prefer to describe it in the same manner that I would define the concept "educational maturity." "Educational maturity is the possession of insight into the significance of the gifts of culture." The special goal of cultural forming is accordingly to instill this insight in people. "Educational maturity" in this instance certainly is not intellectual in nature. "Being culturally formed" is not the equivalent of "knowing much." It means, rather, "having achieved the greatest possible adjustment within the structure of culture in which one lives."

6

Religious Education

RELIGIOUS education is the foundation and principle, it is the objective and the culmination of all education.

The significance of education is primarily religious.

Not a single form of education, not a single act of education may be wholly divested of this religious aspect.

Neither man, nor the life of man, may ever be presented as *diesseitig,* that is, as belonging only to this world.

Even as our entire life is in the hand of God—are not the very hairs of our head numbered?—so we must experience that each moment of our lives is supported by the grace of God and is directed towards the glorification of God.

Up to this point, I am inclined to think, most Christians will be in agreement with me. But perhaps this will no longer be the case when I seek to establish a further relationship between these matters.

That relationship concerns, in the first place, a fact which I have posited repeatedly in these lectures.

In my judgment all human activity can be only as it is because it is the activity of human individuals who are created after the image of God; and consequently it is the action of human beings who possess this religious qualification: they are oriented to the service of God.

In the very structure of thought this essentially religious characteristic comes to the fore or may be said to manifest itself.

Note that this expresses something quite different from the statement that the mind of man reveals "the divine" within him.

The latter expression readily leads to confusion.

Indeed, we are the offspring of God. The fact that we are "the offspring of God" manifests itself in our being religious, and consequently also in our ability to think. But that is something different from stating that the power to reason proves the presence of "the divine" within us.

Although we are the off-spring of God, we are not gods. Not every prince becomes a king. Moreover, we are the fallen children of God. As a result of sin the positive qualities which man possessed before the fall began to have negative effects.

Thus the blood-stream, which in a healthy individual is a life-building stream, becomes a channel of death after a poisonous injection.

It is precisely because we are the off-spring of God that we are capable of sinning. For the same reason our sin can be so cunningly deceitful. And therefore man is evil and guilty, "wholly incapable of doing any good, and inclined to all evil."

However, I do not wish to be misunderstood. Just as man is not divine in nature, so he does not become a devil through sin.

In a certain sense it could be said that man is more than a devil; but in any case he is different.

When God created the world the angels were servants in the great mansion of creation; but man was the child of this household. Now if a servant becomes disloyal to his lord, he is banished from the house and thus the insurrection is put to an end —that is, providing the servant does not succeed in getting the son to rebel against the lord, who is also his father. Now if the son stands up in rebellion against his father, and repudiates his loyalty to his father, then the situation is quite different. Then the break is much more radical. Then the significance of that which has taken place is all the more serious. And this is true not only with respect to the child itself; for now the entire house must bear the consequences of the fall of the son. If this only son is cast out, this then means that a curse comes upon the whole house. In the home the son bore his father's name. The honor of the father in the home was upheld by him. He was the point of contact between the father and the household. But when the son becomes disloyal, a curse falls upon the house: for the sake of man the earth is cursed!

We are here confronted with the most tremendous problem in life. Perhaps it really is the only problem. The problem of sin in the world is, as a matter of fact, the root of all other problems.

Thus we also realize and understand that there is an immediate connection between our view of man as a religious creature and that which we observe to be sinful in man's nature.

Man can be evil only because he is religious in nature. As I have stated before: man alone has a moral existence. His wickedness, his sin reminds us of his nobility. But it is also due to his noble origin that man is capable of such cunning, deceitful wickedness.

We sometimes speak of men being bestial. Now this is foolishness if we mean to say that this bestiality is reminiscent of the animal. A beast cannot be nearly as cunning as a human being. Man, after all, has at his disposal the tremendous apparatus given to him by God for the service of God. He bears the offices of prophet, priest and king. Man possesses a cognitive faculty which enables him to penetrate the deep mysteries which are hidden in the cosmos, the creation of God. In his love and in his self-sacrifice man is capable of expressing something of the miracle of the love of God toward his creation. Man can give expression to something which reminds us of the very being of God.

And man can rule. All things are subjected to him: the most enormous forces of nature, all of technology, even the explosion of the atom-bomb he controls.

But the tragedy of it all is that man no longer is master of his moral majesty. One of the most drastic results of sin is the fact that man's glory has gotten beyond his control.

Man investigates all of creation cognitively and places himself on a pedestal as a prophet only to perish presently in his self-glorification. In love man devotes himself to all that is good and beautiful, but he does not keep in hand this devotion; sooner or later generations of men engage in spiritual suicide by giving their hearts to the mad pursuit of pleasures in which they are radically destroyed. Man begins to dominate, but at the peak of his domination the forces which he has unleashed are directed against man's very existence, because man is incapable of remaining the moral master of those forces. And the world lives in mortal fear of atom-bombs.

Only he who sees this framework of relationships is able to comprehend what enormous problems confront us in religious training.

Religious training is not simply a matter of telling children about the Lord Jesus; it is also a question of showing them in the course of their development from childhood to adulthood how all of life is threatened by the falling away from God.

It is possible to live within creation to the honor of God, to the welfare of self, and in true happiness only if the constantly threatening ruin which is brought on by our own talents can be overcome through fellowship with the cross of Christ. Indeed, in the cross of Christ death was vanquished, and in principle the creational bond between God and the cosmos was restored. No truly new life is possible except through communion with the cross.

Now in religious training the central question is one of the full restoration of man as a matter of principle. The person whom we educate presently must again stand in the world as one who has rediscovered God.

A second fact follows which has decisive significance for our pedagogy and which, therefore, may not be neglected.

A child must learn to think well, for only in this way can he serve the Creator; he must become "a man of culture," because only thus can he seek the honor of God in culture. And so we might go on. Essentially, the matter is as follows: all that we have said about various aspects of education is comprehended in religious education; not only is it embraced in religious education, but it also finds its goal or purpose, its highest significance there.

Let us not be satisfied merely to tell our children that the end of all things is the honor of God, and that life's highest ideal is to serve God. In our task of training we should also guide the child in such a way that he *sees* in us both the actuality and the manner of our glorification of the Creator. By our training we should help the child to learn something of the true meaning of life which can only be found at the place where we meet God in Christ: God who makes us to think and feel and will, who causes our personality to be, who gives us a social community, and who makes us a citizen of the nation in order that we, as His children, may be able to develop our whole self, and simultaneously glorify Him in consequence.

The intent of religious education, therefore, is not first of all the learning of Bible history. To be sure, it is necessary for the Christian to know the word of his Father and to be able to attend to the voice of his Father; it is necessary for him to know in love whatever can be known about the way which the Father has prepared in and through history for the Word which became flesh for our salvation; but, to repeat, that is not the highest significance of religious education.

Nor does it mean that man is to learn much of that which is knowable in the service of God, although that too is required. If God has considered it worth while to tell us about justification and sanctification, and that these two are not identical, then it should be worth our effort to become acquainted with that which the Father discloses to us. If the Father has deemed it important to give us an insight into the nature of our sins and into the manner in which He has wrought deliverance, then we as children shall have to listen gladly and learn what the Father tells us about these matters. Knowledge of these matters is needed if we are going to be able to live as devout Christians. But again, that is not the ultimate import of religious education.

Indeed, the real object of religious training is to enable the child to grow up into an adult, capable of serving his God in every relationship of his God-given place in life, in accordance with the Will and Word of God, in fellowship with Christ, and under the guidance of the Holy Spirit.

This means that the sense of religious training may be comprised in the statement that man must be a suitable instrument to serve God, to do the work of God, to be the child of God in the position given him by God, as well as in the various relationships of life in which God causes him to live.

But then it also immediately becomes clear that the suitability of this instrument is co-determined by the totality of education; and that all of education, in whatever area that may be, and from whatever aspect it be viewed, derives its meaning and value from the fact of man's "being an instrument."

Our evaluation or judgment of a person's life will, in the final analysis, be determined by a single question. That question is: How has this individual performed his Father's work, upheld the honor of his Father, and witnessed to the name of his Father in the world under the divinely controlled circumstances and experiences of his life and in his God-given position in it. That is the only important question which concerns us.

God causes his child to become an existential "fact" within historic and organic processes of development. In the possession of all the talents which the Creator has given him, man may be the child of God; in fact he must be the child of God in this way. Man's suitability for the special task which he must fulfill as a child of God comprises: his reason and his emotion; his will and his social adaptability; his tears and his smile; his character and his temperament; his falling and his rising; his fortune and his misfortune; his failure and his success.

Indeed, God chooses to make man more suited to be his instrument through every experience of life. God uses all of life to whet men into His chiseling tools; but by means of this same life He also forms the tender hands which are needed to do his work.

If we regard general education as the background for religious training, then we still face the problem of determining to what extent we should engage in specifically religious training.

Presumably it will be clear from what we have stated above that we do not mean to suggest that religious training is more or less a separate area of learning which concerns us only on convenient occasions. On the contrary! What we mean is that in addition to the general means given us for the forming of the personality in its totality, God has also given us some special means which we are to employ in religious training.

And when this view is taken, these special means will also very naturally be seen in organic relationship to the usual means of education. These special educational measures will then, as it were, emerge automatically out of the entire life's attitude.

And this I know for certain: a conversation with a child, which arises out of the questions he raises, can be more effective than the memorization of catechism questions by rote. But it does not follow that the memorizing of catechism questions is therefore superfluous.

We shall have to speak separately of these special means and of the inter-relation of these special means with the "structures of life."

For religious training, the knowledge of Bible history is of extremely great importance. That Bible history is the history of salvation.

I have no objection to calling it "the history of the covenant," although that designation may give rise to all kinds of misunderstanding.

Bible history is also "the history of the revelation of God," in and through history. From paradise and the fall to the moment in which the gospel of God goes into the world, the Scriptures depict the course of the revelation of God in life "unhindered" (Acts 28:31).

If an individual truly desires to put into practice his love toward God and His service in this life, then he will have to stand as close as possible to all the things which God made His people to experience as his acts throughout history, and as close as possible to the guidance which He gave to Israel and the direction which He gave to his church.

Never may salvation be divorced from the pathway in which it came to us.

In the Old Testament God reveals himself in his majesty and greatness, and also in his love and loyalty, in accordance with his covenantal promise. The Old and New Testament constitute a unity which is not man-made, but which is inherent, according to the Word of Christ himself.

In our religious training, therefore, we may never make a distinction between the revelation of God in the written Word and the Word which became "flesh." Christ himself said of the Old Testament that these Scriptures bore witness to Him.

For this reason alone it is needful that we present the entire Scriptures to children; and that our children should know thoroughly the history which is presented in the Scriptures in order that they may learn to understand the language of their Father, since only in this way can they approach unto their Savior.

Of course this does not mean that we can expect to develop in children from about six to eight years an understanding of the real and complete significance of the Scriptures. We shall frequently have to tell "Bible history" to younger children as "stories from the Bible." However, these same stories will aid the child in becoming familiar with the revelation of God when he becomes older. In the consciousness of the child these stories gradually merge into a single story, a history, which in reality is also one. It is the task of the elementary school to do everything in its power to have this comprehensive view of the revelation of God, this insight into Bible history, developed in the child by the time he is approximately twelve to fourteen years of age.

Especially in the education of children Bible history will often have to be presented didactically. In passing we may observe that it is very one-sided to state that one should on no occasion make didactic use of the Scriptures, that is to say, that we should never draw a moral or religious lesson from a certain event. The Scriptures do that very thing on a number of occasions. The truth of this will be evident if one but recalls how Elijah is presented as a model or example which teaches very plainly that the fervent prayer of the righteous availeth much. Naturally, in the instruction of our children we must never be satisfied with merely a moral lesson—but that too is obvious from what has been said.

The question of how we are to acquaint the child with Bible history is one of pedagogical practice, and I shall not deal with it at length. I only wish to point out that in telling Bible stories we should adhere as closely as possible to the text of the Bible; but at the same time we ought also to live completely into the child's world of thought and experience.

The child can do nothing more than transfer the content of Bible history as it is presented to him into the framework of his own experience. Not only shall we have to assist the child in doing this, but we shall also have to correct his impressions, if the opportunity presents itself, and if that proves to be necessary.

At a given moment a six-year old in Amsterdam said to his mother: "Mother, I have seen God." As it turned out, this mother was very understanding. She did not immediately say to her child: "Don't be silly," but she asked: "Where did you see God, my child?" Then the child pointed across the street where there was a high house with a window in the top facade. The child said: "He sat there, up high, an old man, with a grey beard." Then the mother acted very intelligently. She did not attempt to explain to the child that God is a spirit, and that He is not therefore an old man with a beard. But realizing that her child was mature enough for another conception, she remarked: "No, my child, then you did not see God, because God lives much higher than that house, very much higher. Look, do you see those clouds? They are much higher than the house, aren't they? Well, God lives even higher than those clouds." This mother realized that she could clarify matters for the child, but she was also aware of the limitations imposed upon her by the age of the child.

Another exceedingly important matter is the general atmosphere we create in telling Bible stories.

In certain circles there once was discussion on the question of the relative importance of spiritual atmosphere and biblical doctrine (*sfeer en leer*). One person wanted to stress atmosphere, another doctrine. The serious discussion of such a contradistinction seems foolishness to me. It is, after all, not a real contrast. For every individual, general atmosphere and doctrinal teaching are one and the same. Even psychologically it is true that the best of doctrine remains without significance for us if the atmosphere or environment in which we receive it affects us adversely or if the atmosphere does not conform to the doctrine; and conversely, atmosphere without anything else will be ineffective. Atmosphere is nothing but an empty form if we do not succeed in bringing into it the doctrine or teaching which belongs there.

It is not my intention to detract from the value of either general atmosphere or of biblical doctrine. Indeed not. Both are of very great significance; really I should say they are inseparable, just as the head and the heart are indivisible. It is true that doctrine makes its appeal to the head, atmosphere to the heart, but taken separately they are ineffective, because the whole personality is not involved. But when atmosphere and doctrine are in complete harmony, then they make their appeal to the child's whole being, and then they will be able to make an impact upon the child in his totality.

Furthermore, the parents and teachers of children between twelve and fifteen years should, when there is an opportunity, relate secular history to sacred, biblical history. The people of the Old Testament, Assyria, Syria, Egypt, and Babylon do not simply appear from nowhere any more than do the Greeks and Romans of the New Testament. It is most desirable to show the children in their training how the nations surrounding Israel played, as it were, "a supporting role" in sacred history, until at last the Roman world-empire had a very great influence at a decisive moment: the fulness of time.

It is equally desirable, even necessary, that children of this age realize that sacred history did not just happen "somewhere," but that it "took place" in a concrete country which they, the students, know. In the upper grades of the elementary school and in the high school a good map of Palestine is indispensable. Pictures and atlases which make the student more conscious of the characteristics of the country can also be of value in this training.

These pictures and atlases can simultaneously serve to familiarize the students with those objects of religious life and daily life in Israel which are mentioned in the Bible repeatedly, since a certain knowledge of these objects is indispensable to the Bible reader.

For example: What is a "threshing-floor?" What did the "table of shew-bread" look like? How should the student picture to himself the "ark of the covenant"? How does "a woman tread a mill"? In summary we may state that in the upper grades of the elementary school and in the high school the teaching of biblical geography and biblical archaeology should, without excessive learnedness, be oriented entirely to the practice of Bible-reading.

That Bible-training in home and school should correspond as closely as possible to the Bible itself is readily understood. A direct contact with the Bible is especially important for children in the upper grades. Part of Bible-training must include developing ability to read the Bible. And the students must continually live in the awareness that the Bible is the source of the knowledge of salvation.

For a teacher to tell a Bible-story without having the Bible before her, as sometimes happens, is psychologically wrong. The children, the little ones included, should not have the feeling that the teacher "is simply telling a nice story." Already at a very early age the children should know at least that the Bible is the source of our knowledge concerning the work of God for our salvation. And as soon as they are able, the children must themselves make use of the Bible. They should be required to read the Bible and to make use of it. They should have to read the Bible at school, but also at home. And at church they should follow the Scripture reading as well as the reading of the text in their own Bibles. In this way we bring the Bible to the child and the child to the Bible.

Not only is Christian education concerned with teaching the Bible, but it also has to take into its purview the truths of faith, the doctrines. The fact that people are not always and everywhere enthusiastic about doctrinal training is probably due largely to the method of teaching. If doctrine or dogma is nothing more than intellectually apprehended truth, which must be drilled into the child until he is able to recite these "truths," then the great danger of schematization and intellectualization threatens religious life. But such a view of doctrine is all wrong.

One who realizes that as a living and believing individual he is in need of attaining the greatest possible comprehension of both God's revelation of Himself, and of man's relationship to God, will also understand that dogma is not a mathematical formulation, but that it is a definition of the truth of God, even as it is a reality in the life of the Christian, and increasingly becomes a greater reality in the daily struggle of faith. For dogma has developed out of the struggle of the church for the truth and against the lie. And as such, dogma is also a description of the struggle of the believer to get ever closer to the truth, that is, to get closer to God. Dogma gives expression to the truth as it grew in the consciousness of believers in the history of the church; but at the same time it also expresses the truth of God which the believer may experience in his own life and in his own heart. Dogma formulates his struggle and his comfort.

Thus dogma is the circumscription of living truth, a reality which can be experienced in the life of the Christian each day.

And whoever comprehends this will likewise understand that Christian education cannot ignore the existence of these doctrines, and that particularly in religious training, dogma has a function of its own.

Now Christian education which has the knowledge of doctrine as its aim is forthwith threatened by two very serious dangers. The first of these dangers is the intellectualism to which we have referred previously. Someone who as a child has learned to rattle off a lesson about the Trinity of God or who recalls in minute detail a lesson about the nature of sin, does not necessarily have respect for the triune God; nor does it follow that he is at all under the impression of the terribleness of sin. The fact that we know much of the truth by no means implies that we love the truth, or that we experience the power of the truth in our heart. The verities of the faith of the church are not mere formulae which are apprehended intellectually; they are definitions of that which God in His grace enabled us to believe and to experience.

But this certainly does not mean that dogma is to be regarded as something which is of no value in education. On the contrary, the danger of dogmatic indifferentism surely is no less than that of intellectualism. For if in intellectualism the danger of petrifaction threatens, it is the danger of indifferentism that man goes to ruin, and that the church dies because of the deadening suction of the morasses of a bottomless subjectivism.

The teaching of the doctrine of faith to children may be compared to walking along a narrow footpath along a mountain ridge. On either side there is a gaping abyss; on the one side it is that of objective intellectualism, on the other that of subjective indifferentism. Education in religion has the task of guiding the child along this narrow path.

Thus we also understand that religious training within this framework is neither an objective relating of the verities of faith, nor a subjective witnessing to that which the educator believes. There must be a simultaneous understanding of head and heart of the truth which God has revealed to us and which has been transmitted to us as the confession of the church in history; it is, moreover, a personal acceptance of, and a personal involvement in this truth, since it is the definition of the content and experience of our personal faith.

In this way religious training indeed retains its objective character, for it is also an objective communication of that which God has told us about himself in relationship to us. But it is something more, too. It is also speaking of what we believe, not because we have been so good to believe it, but because the truth has overcome us in our faith. God has subdued us, with his truth he has overpowered us. But then again, it is also something more, something different, than just speaking of what we have experienced. God says that He desires to overcome us by his truth, and since we have been overcome, his Word has authority for us. To know the verities of the faith, therefore, is also a knowledge of the truth which the Father, as our Father, has made known to us authoritatively. Education in the verities of the faith involves an increasing acquaintance with the Father's words of love, a constantly growing consciousness of that which is present in the heart of the Father, and a mounting jubilation in the awareness that we can find peace in the entire government of our Father, however much we may be "weary and heavy laden."

We and our children may thus understand and experience in religious training something of the riches of the revelation of God.

But whoever understands this, also comprehends that religious training must be oriented to the experiencing of joy in the service of God. Not without reason the Scriptures tell us that we are to rejoice in the Lord, and we are even commanded emphatically: "Rejoice in the Lord; again I say, rejoice."

Assuredly, this happiness is something different than "pleasure," and it is also something other than the constant repetition of "hallelujahs" in which the heart is not present; nor is it gaiety or noisy laughter. It is the joy of a heart which has found rest; it is the rejoicing of a human being who dares and desires to enjoy all the good gifts of God. Children should see in their parents and educators the peace which they have found in Christ.

However, then we shall also have to teach them to understand that the Kingdom of God is not to be found in a negative approach. It is not a question of what you as a Christian may not do. There seemingly are Christians who think a very proper attitude is revealed by the question: "May a Christian do this or that?" Such a question is based on a serious misunderstanding. A Christian may do all things which are not forbidden by God, and he must do all things which God commanded. But this is true for every individual. If God forbids something, then no person may do it. And God's commandments have been given for every individual; they possess the power of law for everyone. Therefore, as children of God, we may never forget: "All things are yours, but you are Christ's, and Christ is God's.

In a truly Christian walk of life, and consequently in education too, the accent may never be placed on what we do and refrain from doing. The stress should fall on what we are, on what we are in our relation to God and to men. The danger is not small that Christians will begin to form a kind of moral code. If you don't do this and don't do that, you may be regarded as a good Christian, living to the honor of God. The Pharisees also possessed such moral codes, and we know how

Jesus satirized them. In Christians of our time, too, it is possible that the outside of the cup is clean, but that the inside is full of venom. There may be Christians who never enter a theater and who expect to be praised accordingly—and perhaps they do deserve that—but who do not hesitate to condemn and malign their fellow Christians without any grounds at all. Our Christian life must be borne by love, even as we ourselves each day again must live and only can live out of the love of God.

People sometimes complain of the critical spirit of young people. But the educators should ask themselves where these young folk learned that spirit of criticism. In Kingdom circles too, the criticism which is felt to be necessary must be in the spirit of love. And not unless our criticism of fellow Christians reveals a loving attitude, which our children can feel and experience, will such criticism be without danger to their religious life. There is one kind of criticism which is particularly dangerous. It is the criticism of those persons who judge their fellow Christians on the basis of what they—the critics—think must be the intent and desire of their fellow Christians, although no such intention or volition has ever been expressed. We may never forget that it is a sin against the ninth commandment "to condemn or to abet the condemnation of a person" on the basis of hearsay. And for religious training such things are disastrous. Our children do not even then see love in our lives. They get the impression that the Christian life is a matter of "following the narrow paths which another prescribes for us"; that it is a matter of "taste not, touch not," of "law upon law and rule upon rule." In Christian education also, very much depends upon the heart of the educator. It is not enough for the educator to be "for the truth." He must also be "behind the truth." Soundness in doctrine is insufficient, for he must be pure in heart, also in his love to his brother and sister. His ability to criticize others is not enough, if he is not able to be critical of himself, first of all. The Christian educator must realize that in his educational task, too, the paradoxically Christian statement holds: "When I am weak, then I am strong."

Therefore, Christian education is possible only where it is supported by daily prayer. And if this paradoxical statement leads us to ask: "Lord, who is equal to these things?" then we hear another word which explains the secret of the Christian educator's life: "I can do all things through Him that strengtheneth me."

The religious basis of his entire existence constitutes the essential nature of man, and so religious training ultimately constitutes the object of all education. Christian education loses its character and core if it does not have as its aim the forming of man as a religious creature in all relationships of life and in all activity.

But then this also implies that the individual, as the servant of God, has a character peculiarly his own in a given time and under given circumstances. Fortunately, the Kingdom of God is such that the possibility of great variations remains. Perhaps it is even a typical sin of some Christians to want to form other individuals "according to their own image and likeness." We should leave that to God who, in the area of religion and of religious life, has desired a seemingly endless variation. The angels praise God for his many-sided wisdom, which is also manifested in his children. Within the circle of the Covenant of Grace and within the circle of those who are loyal to the Word, great variation is possible. The apostle John is a completely different person than is the apostle Peter, and both of these men differ greatly from Paul. Both the manner in which they individually proceed, and the things which they stress in the field of Truth, is very different. And we are bound by God to the truth which is revealed in His Word, not to any individual's point of view, nor to the individual life's attitude of any one of His children. With respect to Christian education, Calvinistic circles may not forget the words of Dr. A. Kuyper: "A mystic inwardness which manifests a glowing ardor for the work of redemption, and which rejoices to walk in the pathway of salvation, is to be preferred to a Christianity which is satisfied with spinning a web of dogma from doctrinal hair-splitting." And we should not forget either what Kuyper added: "The believers of olden days stood on a higher, on a much higher level, when they still understood the truth of 'Learning to know the Lord' in both a doctrinal and a mystical sense. Indeed, from this standpoint God himself remained at the center, and greater, more perfect and more intimate justice was done to religion, which is and remains the 'service' of God."

Whoever comprehends this will also be prevented from absolutizing his own point of view in religious training; he will be kept from a kind of fanaticism which can only be the enemy of all true religion and of all true piety. Even if we maintain the full and distinctive value of the Reformed confession, we will still have an eye for the grace of God given in it, and further we will see that there are hundreds of thousands of Christians who —although not accepting our confession—nevertheless, in many very important points of doctrine, perhaps even in the most important points of doctrine, stand beside Reformed believers in the hosts of the Kingdom of Christ. Our religious training should be such, that when necessary our children do not shun isolation, but conversely, may be free from all false zealotry; that they may acknowledge the bond of fellowship with brothers and sisters with whom they will be routed into the same corner by the antichrist at the end of days; and that they do this because these brothers and sisters also acknowledge King Jesus as their Savior with their whole heart.

In this way only can religious training constitute the true basis for the ethical forming of the personality to which we referred earlier. Only thus can the church of Christ be built without running the danger of narrowing into a sect. Thus, and only thus, will Christian education have the assurance of never losing the child, nor of ever losing the Cross of Christ.

In this way Christian education of the present receives a stimulus from the entire sacred past, and in this way it teaches the children to look forward to the future coming of Jesus Christ. And thus it also teaches the children to pray: "Come, Lord Jesus, yea, come quickly."